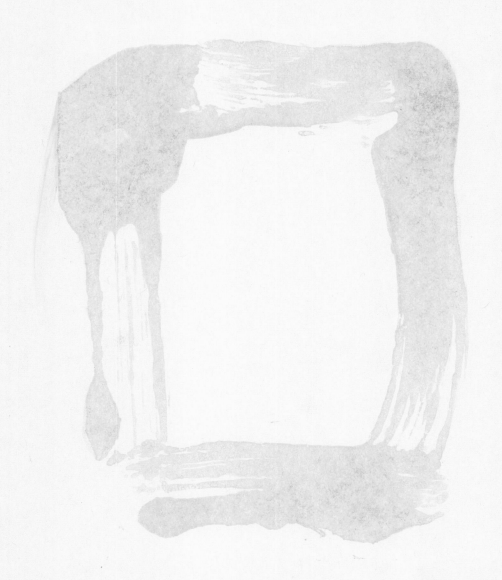

VAN GOGH

1 Cypresses, June 1889.
Metropolitan Museum of Art, New York.

VAN GOGH

FREDERICK S. WIGHT

FORTY-SIX REPRODUCTIONS
INCLUDING
TWELVE IN FULL COLOR

THE BEECHHURST PRESS NEW YORK

PUBLISHED BY THE BEECHHURST PRESS
11 EAST 36TH STREET, NEW YORK 16, N. Y.

FIRST EDITION

ILLUSTRATIONS

Color

Acknowledgments

The publishers wish to thank the following for making photographs available (numbers refer to illustrations): Soichi Sunami, Museum of Modern Art, 1, 2, 4, 5, 8, 13, 14, 17, 22, 26, 28; Metropolitan Museum of Art, 3, 9, 31, 32, 34, I; Art Institute of Chicago, 6, 27, VI; J. K. Tannhauser, New York, 7; Fogg Museum of Art, 10, 16; George Flipse, Arnheim, V; Wildenstein Gallery, 12; National Gallery of Art, Washington, D. C., 15; Victor Amato, Washington, D. C., 20; John Harvey Heffren, New York, 21, 33; Peter A. Juley & Son, New York, 23; Knoedler Gallery, 29; Cleveland Museum of Art, 30; Oliver Baker, New York, II, IV, IX; Museum of Fine Arts, Boston, III, VIII, XI, XII; Minneapolis Institute of Arts, X; Three Lions, New York, VII.

VINCENT VAN GOGH

I.

Vincent van Gogh has written a biography in his self-portraits. Severity, self-mortification, prideful humility and ever-latent defiance; the coming anxiety as his hopes failed him, the expression moving through suspicion to anger to desolation—all are here. Here too is his work-a-day appearance, the rough calloused shell of his life which he had grown as a sign of his self-demotion from the worthy professional class into which he was born. For he wished to prove himself one of the poor, and he showed himself in all his acquired coarseness: spiky, rude and stark. We see him well along on his road to self-abasement in his search for salvation and peace of mind.

He came of a family in which respectability was synonymous with self-respect. The van Goghs had identified themselves with the arts and with the church. Vincent's father, Theodorus, was a clergyman, a good mild man lacking the eloquence to lift himself out of a rural parsonage. He ministered first at Groot-Zundert on the southern border of Holland, where Vincent was born. Later he removed to Etten, and then to Nuenen: modest callings, changes rather than advancements—worthiness was the claim of Theodorus van Gogh. The painter's grandfather, likewise Vincent van Gogh, was also a clergyman, but a man who loomed in the world. He ministered at Breda. He had twelve children, four sons elder to Theodorus, who all out-figured the country pastor. Of these uncles to our Vincent, the eldest, Jan, became a Vice-Admiral. The next three were art dealers: Heinrich at Rotterdam, Cornelius at Amsterdam, and Uncle Vincent, junior partner—before his retirement—in the important Paris firm of Goupil which had branch offices at The Hague and in London.

For three dim generations behind the grandfather clergyman at Breda the van Goghs had been goldsmiths. Then there was a Vincent van Gogh in the eighteenth century, a sculptor who had first lifted the family into prominence: so our painter was fourth of the name. It was Uncle Vincent, however, whose career pointed the way. Rich, retired, and ailing, he lived a carriage-drive away at Princenhage, not too far from his father at Breda or his brother Theodorus at Etten. His home was full of splendid things and he went to Mentone for the winter. Childless, he would drive over to see his nieces and nephews. Vincent was his name-

sake. It was not strange that the pastor should look to his brother Vincent for preferment for his sons.

Our Vincent was born on March 30, 1853, a year to a day after a still-born first son. There were six children in all, Vincent, then a girl, then Theo, named for his father and four years younger than Vincent, then two girls and one more son. It was Vincent and Theo whose lives were to interlock, the painter leaning on his younger brother all his days, writing him volumes of letters, building up such an interdependence, one brother somehow providing significance for the other to a degree more usually associated with marriage, so that their deaths fell only a few months apart.

It was hoped that both boys would be art dealers, and sure enough when Vincent was sixteen Uncle Vincent advised him to enter Goupil's, and Theo's turn came in due course. Vincent was taken on at The Hague branch as the youngest and doubtless most favored employee, under the personal care of the manager Tersteeg. Vincent's foot was on the carpeted stair—but it was Theo who would make the climb.

Vincent was at The Hague for three years. Before he left, Theo, then fifteen, came to visit him. There were walks with an old mill for destination and musings on the flat infinities of Holland under a transcendent sky. In the last two years German armies had been sweeping westward and capturing Paris, but this was far beyond their peaceful horizon. The young men were full of adolescent obliviousness, full of mystic dedications and yearnings after righteousness: they meant to be worthy of their clergyman father. When Theo left, Vincent wrote him the first of the hundreds of letters which were to survive.

When Vincent was twenty he was transferred to Goupil's London office. He had letters of introduction, a salary sufficient for modest savings, and a top hat. He boarded with two ladies who kept two parrots, but soon—with his instinct for moving down in the world—he found a cheaper place and lived with a clergyman's widow. This Mrs. Loyer kept a school for little children with her daughter Ursula. It was not long before Vincent was in love with Ursula and writing his sister to "love her for my sake." But as it turned out, Ursula was engaged, and he was at once rejected. It was only a rebuff

1 Carpenter's Work Shop and Laundry, drawing, 1882.
Kröller-Müller State Museum, Otterlo.

of first love, yet it had its consequences and it had its sequels. It was in Vincent's nature to make imperious demands which could never be satisfied. His devotions were to maintain the desperate sincerity of first love together with first love's lack of any sure base, its vulnerability to ridicule and disaster. Vincent moved out of the house. He was transferred to the Paris office; but after a few months he was back in London.

Vincent's divergence from the usual now began, and he began to disappoint expectations. He was interested in painting, yes, but not as a dealer. Buying and selling, the whetting of appetites, the obsequious inflections of "yes," were distasteful to his nature. He turned in on himself. He drew a little, he read much, and he moralized. His amiable and successful Uncle Vincent had to warn him that mixing with people was just as necessary as learning business. But Vincent was shifting his ground. He was seeking less worldly values, and soon he was in flight from the crassness of his employment. He was turning from art to religion.

Just as Vincent was to battle with his family without ever emerging from family dependence, he never departed from his family's two destinies, art

and theology. He simply transferred allegiance from one to the other, from art to religion and again back to art, until in the end he managed to fuse them, at some white heat, into an art that was also a gospel.

The art appreciation of his time wallowed in sentimental content. Yet making every allowance for the time, Vincent's early tastes are a prey to the pathetic, and so they were to remain. He liked Rembrandt, he liked Millet, and he liked Jules Breton. What had the greatest and the least in common?—the peasant theme. He liked the anecdotal Gérome and Meissonier. The truth was that he judged works of art in terms of the morality or humanity, obvious or profound, and he bowed his head before Millet because the peasants were bareheaded at the sound of the angelus.

In his literary taste the canon was the same. He read Dickens, he read George Eliot, and he brought the same earnest response to Harriet Beecher Stowe. French writers presented more of a problem. Here Vincent, son of a Dutch country clergyman, recoiled from the Gallic freedom which seemed to be limited or defined not by morality but by style. Totally innocent in his behavior, a sense of guilt stirred

8

2 Old Man with Bowed Head, drawing, 1882.
Kröller-Müller State Museum, Otterlo.

in his mind. Michelet the chronicler of the French Revolution preyed upon him to the point of book burning. Renan, the historian and renegade priest, stirred him greatly. Later, in more emancipated days, he read Zola, but he read him with a religious fervor for the humanity he found.

The spiritual quest of the young man of twenty-two was leading down a familiar Protestant path, however solitary it seemed: the path to exaltation and wonder before the natural and the supernatural, marked out for the nineteenth century by the conscience-ridden Carlyle. Nothing could be further afield from the suavities of art dealing. A concerted effort to rescue Vincent was in order and he was once more transferred to headquarters, to the Paris house.

If not a promotion, perhaps this at least would be a solution. It was May of the year 1877. Vincent lived on Montmartre. Paris spread wide before him and below him in all its complexity, its moral shadings as disturbingly various as the personalities here hidden yet scurrying—all hoping to prosper under the new Republic, the city itself endlessly awake and dazzling by gaslight. The history of art, which was his business by family right, was as deep and wide as the history of the city, as current as the morning paper, a paraphrase of all that had happened or went on before him. And that was what was the matter. Something was wrong, something was tainted. For if it had been so difficult to sift right from wrong in London, how was it to be possible here?

9

3 The Loom, May 1884.
Kröller-Müller State Museum, Otterlo.

Vincent had appeared eccentric in London as he grew more angular with unpleasant virtues. How was it to be in this most citified of cities? He was assigned permanent duty in the Goupil picture gallery where he was expected to grow smoother and more urbane as he lived in contact with the public. "The path is narrow . . . we must be careful," he wrote his brother. "Work and pray. God will give good gifts . . . that will not be taken away . . . I am going to destroy all my books by Michelet. I wish you would do the same . . . How I long for Christmas"—it was September—"but let us have patience; it will come soon enough."

He had for roommate a young Englishman—or boy—Harry Gladwell, who also worked at Goupil's. Gladwell was eighteen, and since he was soon to take the place of the gauche and unpliable Vincent it is touching that he first struck Vincent as uncouth.

Vincent was still far from his peasant guise, and Gladwell had "strong teeth . . . glittering eyes . . . projecting ears, close-cropped head"—curiously, a future portrait of Vincent himself. In the evening Vincent read Longfellow or the Bible aloud, and in the morning Gladwell prepared the oatmeal sent to him in bulk by his father. Gladwell had never been away before and he "had a sickly (though noble) longing for his father and his home . . . a longing that belongs only to God and to Heaven."

Both young men acted on their desires and went to their homes for Christmas. This was the season of the year when Vincent's presence was needed most acutely in the gallery, and it was either the reason or the excuse for his separation from the firm. Uncle Vincent or no Uncle Vincent, when he returned he was discreetly discharged and he left in March. Gladwell had already moved away from

10

II Portrait of the Artist with Easel, 1888.
Collection V. W. Van Gogh, Laren.

11

him, as people did. Vincent wondered if Gladwell would come back to their old room, and as Gladwell was to take his place in the art gallery, Vincent had the task of familiarizing him with the job. This he did utterly without rancor; Vincent knew how ill-suited he was for the place.

So the career for which Vincent had been prepared was at an end, and he began to grope his way ahead by improvisation. He had been reading advertisements in the English papers, and he accepted a temporary place without salary with an English schoolmaster at Ramsgate. After a period of trial for Vincent Mr. Stokes was to decide whether he was fit for the position. Vincent had turned from art dealer to teacher as the first step in a new life of dedication and good works.

A Dickensian interlude now unfolded. Spartan meagerness characterized Mr. Stokes' boarding school. Here Vincent seemed no older than his twenty-four charges. He was certainly as innocent, and no more comfortable. If he were seeking poverty and a drab escape from temptation it was provided. Yet he could hardly live on nothing, and nothing his salary remained all the time he was with Mr. Stokes. In his new narrow circumstances the religious current in him began to run deeper and stronger, love of God sweeping him into the stream of humanity and making men his brothers whether they knew it or not; love of nature welling in him out of all that remained from his appreciation of works of art. The Turneresque scenes about him went into his letters: the storms, the low torn skies, the pale green churn of the North Sea, and the heavy surf pounding against the seawall that fronted the bleak little town. From now on he painted landscapes in words, and this verbal expression was to remain in full spate even after he began to paint furiously on canvas. One may speculate on the objective health his letters provided his painting, siphoning off as they did the literary side of his endowment.

Young Theo was already getting on, and unconsciously Vincent had to look up as he looked back. "I am so glad that we have so many things in common, not only memories of childhood but also that you are working in the same house in which I was till now and know so many people and places which I know also, and that you have so much love of nature and art."

Vincent, lonely at Ramsgate, wished to go up to London. He had no money, so he went on foot. He went to see his sister who was employed in London. "She is looking well and you would like her little room as I do, with the 'Good Friday,' 'Christ in the Garden of Olives,' 'Mater Dolorosa' framed in ivy." He went also, out of loneliness, to see the Gladwells, and left with no other thought

than that it might be given him to prove his friendship for their son.

A few months more and Vincent hastened to see Harry Gladwell who was home from Paris for a few days. The circumstances had in them something of the Vincent to come, the putting up of a muddy paw with desperate fidelity. Gladwell's young sister had been killed suddenly in a fall from a horse. Vincent heard of the tragedy and set out on a six hours' walk which brought him to the Gladwells just as the family was returning from the funeral. "It was indeed a house of mourning and it was good to be with them . . . I had a long talk with Harry until late that evening, about all kinds of things, about the Kingdom of God and about the Bible, and talking thus we walked up and down the station, and I think we shall never forget those last moments before we said good-bye."

Mr. Stokes had moved his school to Isleworth, but there was still no prospect of salary for his helper. Vincent had a further reason to detach himself; he wished now to preach as well as to teach, and he became an assistant, "a sort of curate," to a Methodist minister, Mr. Jones. He was to preach one sermon only, and he chose for his text: "I am a stranger upon earth, hide not thy commandments from me." The church where he preached was at Petersham and Vincent made a drawing of the building in order to describe it.

Vincent now had been in England from April until November. He had a day off, and again he set forth to see the world afoot. He left home at four in the morning so that he was in Hyde Park by half past six, then to Whitechapel, Chancery Lane and Westminster, with a side excursion to see Mrs. Loyer, mother of the unforgotten Ursula, and on to Lewisham to see the Gladwells, where he plodded in at half-past three. It was just three months since their little daughter was buried. "I spent about three hours with them and many were the thoughts that came to us all . . ." By half-past ten he was back home.

Where to turn and where to trudge, now that his one sermon was delivered? "If ever you have the opportunity of reading Bunyan's *Pilgrim's Progress*, you will find it worth your while." For he was copying texts out of the book to comfort the Gladwells. The pilgrim went home again for Christmas and once more it was time for the family to take a hand. There was no point in his returning to England—he never did return—and something else had to be found. Some simple unambitious solution, nearer at hand. "As to the religious work, I still do not give it up . . . The change will be that instead of teaching the boys, I shall work in a bookshop." This bookshop proved to be one of the briefest solutions of all.

4 Peasant Woman Binding a Sheaf, drawing, 1883-85.
Kröller-Müller State Museum, Otterlo.

II.

Vincent's relations lived in the midst of faith, but Vincent now turned to religion with a fervor which disconcerted them. "You think he is more than an ordinary human being, but I think it would be much better if he thought of himself as just an ordinary human being," his sister wrote to Theo. "I wish he could find some work in connection with art or nature," said his mother. The bookstore at Dordrecht was certainly not the right employment. Unaware that he had already preached his first and last sermon, Vincent still burned to become a clergyman like his father and grandfather before him.

It was settled finally that he was to be properly trained in theology. By May of the new year—it was now 1878—Vincent went to live with his Uncle Jan, Commandant of the Navy Yard at Amsterdam. His preliminary plunge into poverty had been in the name of religion and it meant as yet no break with respectability. Another uncle found a teacher for him. At this stage he would only be studying for the state examination which would admit him to the University. He had a long road ahead. How long would it be before he could be a clergyman—and what if Vincent had known he had but thirteen years to live? "Oh Theo, Theo boy, if I might only succeed in this, if that heavy depression because everything I undertook failed, that torrent of reproaches which I have heard and felt, if it might be taken from me..." But this meant fortitude and patience. "My head is sometimes heavy and often it burns and my thoughts are

13

5 *The Potato Eaters, May 1885.*
Collection V. W. Van Gogh, Laren.

confused . . . Regular study after all those emotional years is not always easy."

Solitary walks, the city, the dusk, the graveyard, the infinity of flat landscape—nature was now loved for its religious significance. "There is much evil in the world and in ourselves, terrible things . . ." Recollection, nostalgia, times when he and Theo were together, the heartbreak deepening. He had an unquenchable appetite for sermons. But underneath there was a constant concern for art, a hankering after paintings and prints. And suddenly there was a shy blossoming of happiness. "When I am writing I instinctively make a little drawing, now and then, like the one I sent you lately, and for instance, this morning, Elijah in the desert, with the stormy sky, and in the foreground a few thorn bushes, it is nothing special but I see it all so vividly before me . . ."

His interest in paintings and prints was now unabashedly moral. But it was also restlessly alive.

His Uncle Cornelius—the dealer here in Amsterdam —had a home and gallery open to Vincent. It was he who presented Vincent with Bossuet's Funeral Orations. But when Uncle Cor asked Vincent whether he did not like Gerome's *Phryne*— was he mocking his nephew or trying to soften his austerity?—in any case he was in for a rebuff. "I told him I would rather see a homely woman by Israëls or Millet, or an old woman by Edouard Frère; for of what use is such a beautiful body as that of Phryne, the animals have it too . . ." Uncle Cor, however, persisted, and asked Vincent if he should feel no attraction for a beautiful woman or girl, and got a plain answer. "I told him I would feel more attraction for, and would rather come in contact with one who was ugly, or old, or poor, or in some way unhappy, but who through experience and sorrow, had gained a mind and a soul." At this time Vincent was copying out by hand Thomas à Kempis' *Imitation of Christ.*

14

III Postman Roulin, August 1888.
Collection Robert T. Paine, 2nd, Boston.

How to reach suffering humanity? Was there no short cut, so that his own suffering could be joined directly to that of others? There was in Vincent a desperate, a justified, impatience with time. It corresponded to the sweep and surge toward the far horizon in his painting, the flat distance exaggerated, as it is in the mind of a child left behind. His father came to visit him. When his father left he was going no great distance, nor was it an inevitable separation, yet for Vincent—"when I had seen father off at the station, and had looked after the train as long as it was in sight, even the smoke of it, and came home to my room and saw father's chair still standing near the little table on which the books and copybooks of the day before were still lying, though I know that we shall see each other again pretty soon, I cried like a child."

"There are so many, many things, one has to know." As he grew restless, he believed he had stumbled on a by-pass to all this learning and study. He had the few-great-works-of-history idea. How much knowledge was needed for wisdom? "A knowledge of history in general and of certain persons from all ages, especially from the history of the Bible to that of the (French) Revolution, and from the Odyssey to the books of Dickens and Michelet." One could learn from artists too, and here followed Vincent's confraternity of the painters of peasants: Rembrandt, Millet and Breton.

15

The theological road came to look desperately long. He might be on the towpath of a canal, with the people he wished to help on the opposite bank, and the next bridge almost out of sight. A rationalization was building up. Faith, good works and poverty were the short-cut to godliness. "Whoever lives sincerely and encounters much trouble and disappointment, but is not bowed down by them, is worth more than one who has always sailed before the wind and has only known relative prosperity." Salvation was all about him; it was the poor who lived in God.

"Laborers, your lot is sad, you have lives of suffering, you are the blessed." Vincent was preparing himself for another act of rejection. He would not be an ordained minister but rather a missionary. Thus he would not have to face competing with his father or his grandfather, and at the same time he would triumph over them by being more humble than both.

"I am writing you by the light of a little lantern, and the candle is getting too short." Vincent had now given up his hopes of the University, he had left Amsterdam, doubtless to the Admiral's relief, and his family's plans for him were growing simpler through despair. Home at Etten for the summer, he was set on a humbler and nearer goal, he was headed for a training school for evangelists in Brussels.

At the school he found himself older, more advanced, than the other students; but at the conclusion of the three months' course he failed to receive his appointment. This was unforeseen, an overwhelming defeat which Vincent's stubbornness would by no means accept. The best compromise was to let him go along on his own regardless, with his father's consent and support. He was sleepless and weak; it was too late, indeed dangerous, to thwart him.

It was Vincent's ambition to become a missionary among the miners in the coalfields of southern Belgium and northern France, a depressed region called the Borinage. Here was an opportunity for humility, enough to set even Vincent's conscience at rest. Vincent of course wished to share this ambition with Theo and he wrote of his future plans enclosing a sketch—as if in anticipation—of a desolate little pothouse, *The Coalpit*. This drawing—"it is nothing indeed"—was recognizably a van Gogh in terms of what was to come. It was all van Gogh up to date too: humility a-plenty, twilight without and light within, keyed to the emotions of a belated—or benighted—child. The long and fervent word-painting was now breaking down into the actual image. It was no longer enough to refer to Rembrandt, Millet or Breton. Descriptions and analogies were too remote. Vincent had to offer the actual sight of what he had seen.

That winter he saw the Borinage. He boarded in humble circumstances enough, teaching his landlord's children in the evening. He visited the sick and poor, gave Bible readings, and drew maps of Palestine, selling four to his father at ten francs each. He went down into the most dangerous mine of the region. Literally he submerged himself with these people, his need for humanity satiated at last, their poverty his humility. "Most of the miners are thin and pale from fever and look tired and emaciated, weather-beaten and aged before their time, the women as a whole faded and worn. Around the mine are poor miners' huts with a few dead trees black from smoke, and thorn hedges, dung hills, and ash dumps, heaps of useless coal, etc. . . . I will try to make a little sketch of it presently to give you an idea of how it looks."

He received after all a belated and begrudging nomination as an evangelist—for six months. He had plenty to do. ". . . there have been cases of typhoid and malignant fever, of what they call 'the mad fever,' that gives them bad dreams like nightmare, and makes them delirious." But in the midst of all this there were questions about painting, questions about the Dutch painters Israëls and Anton Mauve, whom Theo knew at The Hague. "Have you seen some beautiful pictures lately?" Vincent asked wistfully, for he was seeing no paintings at all.

It was not long before Vincent was pushing Christian humility to its ultimate extreme. He had copied out the *Imitation of Christ*. Acts of sainthood were simple events to him, but they were not in the Protestant scheme of sainthood which involved a respect for vested property—or how could charity be maintained? "With the charcoal burners one must have a charcoal burner's character and temperament, and no pretentious pride or mastery, or one would never get on with them or gain their confidence." So he left his boardinghouse and went to live in a miner's hut. He gave away his money, his clothes, his bed. This was not the example desired by the Church Council at Wasmes. The Council met: if Vincent did not listen to reason he would lose his position. "Jesus was also very calm in a storm," Vincent commented. Vincent's father had to come on the scene to soothe the committee and bring his son back to the boardinghouse. A mine explosion and a strike gave Vincent employment and doubtless took the attention of the committee from him. But by summer the committee had got round to him again. It was obvious that nothing would change him and he was discharged with three months notice. The solution was to live once more on his own—that is, on his family—in the Borinage, and so he boarded with an evangelist in the village of Cuesmes.

16

6 Montmartre, 1886-88.
Art Institute of Chicago.

By now he had begun to make sketches of the miners to show his family when he came home. This sketching and drawing continued through the winter, and he became less of an evangelist. He had lost hope in this way of life, and with this hope he lost his orthodox faith. Religious texts faded out of his letters which ceased to be sermons. He was beginning to trust and record experience. It was a time of change.

He was often destitute. Support from home was meager and intermittent, and uneven support was unevenly spent, money slipping childishly through his hands. Yet the time when he was a fledgling student in Amsterdam seemed far worse to him: "...the worst time I ever lived through. How

desirable and attractive have become the difficult days, full of care here in this poor country, in these uncivilized surroundings, compared to that...

I would rather die a natural death than to be prepared for it by the Academy, and I sometimes have had a lesson from a hay-mower that was of more use to me than one in Greek."

Finally there was a letter to Theo, written in July of 1880: "I learned at Etten that you sent fifty francs for me, well I have accepted them. Certainly with reluctance, certainly with a rather melancholy feeling, but I am up against a stone wall, and in a sort of mess." From now on he was to live in the shelter of another wall he was up against—Theo's support.

7 The Bridge across the Seine, 1886.
Collection J. K. Tannhauser, New York.

Vincent's need eventually became an imperious demand, and his hold on Theo became his hold on his own sanity, his one sure bond with the outer world. He was to exasperate, burden, torment Theo, inviting a rejection of which he knew there was no risk. At the same time this relationship, this support was to focus Vincent on art. For Theo was a dealer who could turn art into money. Very well, Vincent would make restitution, would pay back with drawings, paintings . . . Eventually this exchange became so rationalized and established that Vincent could refuse to admit a debt to Theo when his conscience hurt him too much. So Theo, allowing Vincent to impose upon him, became the banker who bought up the sense of guilt which plagued Vincent. And by painting faster and faster Vincent strove to pay off this sense of guilt in search of his peace of mind. This whole cycle would take ten years to run, the ten years Vincent and Theo still had to live.

In 1880 Vincent had little to offer Theo but his letters; he was just beginning to draw. But he knew that change lay ahead. "What moulting time is for birds—the time when they change their feathers—so adversity or misfortune is . . . for us human beings. One can stay in it, in that time of moulting, one can also come out of it renewed, but anyhow it must not be done in public and . . . the only thing to do is to hide oneself."
Something was brewing, some self-realization. His need for humility was for the moment appeased. A sense of worth was arising within him, regardless of how he was employed. ". . . I have often neglected my appearance, this I admit, and I admit that it is shocking. But look here, poverty and want have their share in the cause, and then a deep discouragement comes in too for a part, and then it is sometimes a good way to assure oneself the necessary solitude for concentration on some study that preoccupies one." This winter he made a long

18

IV Sunflowers, August 1888.
Collection V. W. Van Gogh, Laren.

expedition afoot to Courrières in the north of France in the hope of seeing Jules Breton. But he only saw the outside of the new studio of the man he so admired, and he drew away disheartened, lacking the courage to make himself known. Yet his journey had broken a miasma, had established a direction and published a need, if only to himself. He had returned to his first direction. He had swung from art to religion and now back to art.

His beginnings as an artist were steeped in his native humility. He copied Millet. He turned toward Theo, asking for more prints to copy. But if he was to be an artist he had to see paintings again; he must also see his fellows—he was neither peasant nor miner after all. He had known Paris, and Theo was in Paris. Yet there was some force which held the brothers at a distance from each other as surely as it held them together. As a compromise, Vincent went to Brussels—which he also knew—and took a room in a small hotel.

III.

Theo sent Vincent more than money, he sent him a friend. A young Dutch painter named van Rappard had come from Paris to Brussels to study at the Academy and Theo gave Vincent an introduction. Vincent presented himself in van Rappard's room at nine in the morning. Van Rappard was rich and titled and there was a considerable gap to cross. Yet van Rappard responded to Vincent's sincerity and need; he offered him the use of his studio, and became his friend. Outside of Theo Vincent had hardly another. The friendship lasted for five difficult years and was broken from Vincent's side.

The Academy offered Vincent what it had to offer: anatomy and perspective. Vincent also hired private models daily—"an old porter or a working man"—which took all his money. Drawing types of working people would lead, he hoped, to doing illustrations for papers and books. He had his eye on the work of Gavarni and Daumier. He had his eye too on Paris, but at what a distance. "As you vaguely spoke to me some time ago about coming to Paris, I must tell you that I wish no better than to go there some day soon, if I were sure of finding work that would give me at least a salary of 100 francs a month..."

Money: Vincent learned from his parents that Theo had been sending far more money for him than he realized. Vincent took it up with Theo, desperately trying to spread the burden. "...in a family like ours, where two Messrs. van Gogh are very rich, and both in the line of art, Uncle Cor and our Uncle of Prinsenhage (Uncle Vincent), and where

of the younger generation, you and I have chosen the same line, though in different spheres, would it be well, I say, if this being so, I should not be able to count on 100 francs a month for the time that must necessarily elapse before I can get regular work as a draftsman?" He had unfortunately quarreled with Uncle Cor, but that should be no excuse for Uncle Cor to desert him. And he complained that outsiders took their cue from his family, and gave him a chilly reception because he was under a cloud at home.

And yet, with summer coming on again, the virtues of returning home and living expense free loomed to him, as they do to such prisoners. "The cheapest way would perhaps be for me to spend this summer at Etten..."

The summer at home brought a new difficulty that Vincent had largely escaped. Humility and poverty had kept him out of the way of love and marriage. There had been Ursula, years ago. But when he was in Amsterdam he had denied to Uncle Cor the attraction of Phryne. When he was in the Borinage he gave away his money and his bed, and doubtless sacrificed still more to his conscience. But now his views were changing. He was to be an artist, and he had his claim to happiness. As a human being he had his minimal rights.

The summer at Etten, being a change and a return, began auspiciously enough. Van Rappard paid him a visit—and the presence of his well-bred friend could not have hurt Vincent's standing at home. Theo returned from Paris, and that was a joy. And a cousin K arrived from Amsterdam, older than Vincent, recently widowed, with a young son. Vincent now fell under the spell of this older cousin. There were walks, and little attentions. Vincent devoted himself to the child—he loved children—but it did not serve to win the mother. There are childlike temperaments which attract children and repel women simultaneously—one thinks at once of Hans Christian Andersen. Vincent asked his question and received "no" for an answer, as he had from Ursula. The widow tactfully recalled her devotion to the dead.

Humility in Vincent never went counter to a stubborn pursuit of his desires: the genius and neurotic have in common the lengths they will go to obtain their wishes. He persisted, and the "no" became a firm "no, never." Cousin K's position grew embarrassing, and she concluded her visit and returned to Amsterdam. But Vincent was by no means defeated. He wrote to Theo about the state of his heart.

"What kind of love was it I felt when I was twenty? It is difficult to define, my physical passions were very weak then, perhaps because of a few years of great poverty and hard work. But my intellectual

8 Self-Portrait, 1886-88.
Collection Mr. and Mrs. Joseph Winterbotham, Burlington, Vermont.

passions were strong ... without asking anything in return, without wanting any pity, I only wanted to give, but not to receive. Foolish, wrong, exaggerated, proud, rash, for in love one must not only give but also take ..." If he wrote to Theo you may be sure he wrote to K. His parents were confronted with the situation; so was the outer circle of his relations. Only Uncle Vincent somewhat sardonically encouraged his nephew to persist.

At the parsonage there was now unhappiness and anxiety. Vincent quarreled with his father, attacking the minister's conventionality—for is not convention the enemy of true morality? "When father

V Portrait of the Artist (dedicated to Gauguin), October 1888.
Fogg Museum of Art, Wertheim Collection, Cambridge, Mass.

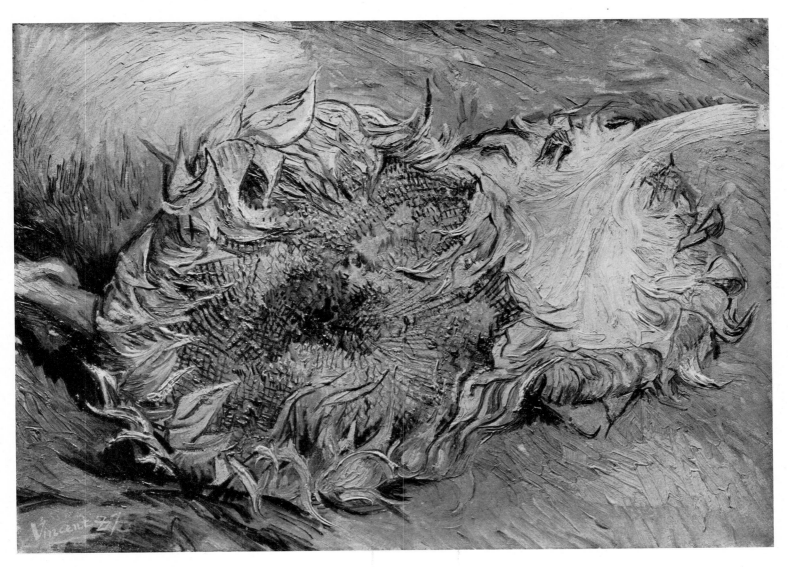

9 Sunflowers, 1887.
Metropolitan Museum of Art, New York.

sees me with a French book by Michelet or Victor Hugo, he thinks of thieves and murderers, or of 'immorality,' but this is too ridiculous . . . So often I have said to father, just read a few pages . . . but father obstinately refuses to do so . . . Just now while this love nestled into my heart, I read anew the book by Michelet, *L'Amour et la Femme*, and so many things became clear to me that otherwise would have been riddles. I told father frankly . . . that I attached more value to the advice of Michelet than to his own . . . But they bring up the story of a great uncle who was infected with French ideas, who took to drink, and so they insinuate that I will follow his career."

Vincent acquainted K's parents with his desire. Knowing their attitude in advance, he sent her father a "very undiplomatic letter" by registered mail, so that there could be no doubt that it reached its mark. His rejection was categoric; nevertheless he went to Amsterdam, obtained entrance into K's house, and confronted her father. But he failed to obtain sight of K. This was the occasion when he held his hand in the flame of a candle to prove his earnestness, asking to see K for only as long as he continued to hold his hand in the flame.

It was December, the end of 1881. The days were short and gray and the atmosphere at the parsonage was black. Doubtless his parents saw no end in view, and when Vincent himself could bear it no longer, he flung off for The Hague. The final conflict in his mind when he left was whether it was right to leave with his work incomplete, his drawings of the Brabant types in the vicinity. For his art had already become an obligation. His drawings were no longer to show at home, or to show to Theo. They existed in their own right. His art was becoming a way of life, which would gather force as other outlets were denied him.

"Carpenter's Workshop and a Laundry" (fig. 1) shows how he provided for himself.

"I have rented a studio here, there is a room with an alcove that can be arranged for that purpose,

23

10 Three Pairs of Shoes, 1886–88.
Fogg Museum of Art, Wertheim Collection, Cambridge, Mass.

cheap enough, on the outskirts of the town, on the Schenweg." "Carpenter's Workshop and a Laundry" gives us a glimpse of the environment, shows too the meticulous fidelity of his early drawing. His work retained to the end the unquiet intensity of perspective, the sweep off into space.

As always, with a change of direction his spirits rose. An impossible situation had given place to something feasible once more. He had the city where he had spent his first three years away from home; he had the museum and the Rembrandts; and the friendship—in the beginning—of the older painter Anton Mauve whom he admired. But he had only been in The Hague a month when he became involved with a woman whom he hired to pose, and established a relationship which was to scandalize relatives and friends alike. "Bad connections often arise from a feeling of loneliness," said his father sadly. Vincent played a part curiously compounded of Christian charity and Bohemianism; by his generosity to the woman he was able to

outrage his father and mother and to insult the memory of his rejected love.

His discovery, Christine, had little to recommend her. Vincent found her in the street; she was sick and pregnant, and she already had a child. She had a mother of sorts in the background, pregnant with ill advice. Vincent took Christine in, nursed her, took her to a maternity hospital in Leyden when her time came. Vincent himself was ill and in the hospital with some inflammatory condition while Christine, or Sien, as she was called, was having her child. And Vincent accepted the infant boy as if he were his own.

It was March before Theo knew of the course on which Vincent had embarked. ". . . you have my bread in your hands," Vincent challenged him defiantly, "will you take it from me, or turn your back on me? Now I have spoken and await what further will be said to me." Theo did not turn his back. From now on his role became really difficult. He could not quarrel with Vincent, because every-

24

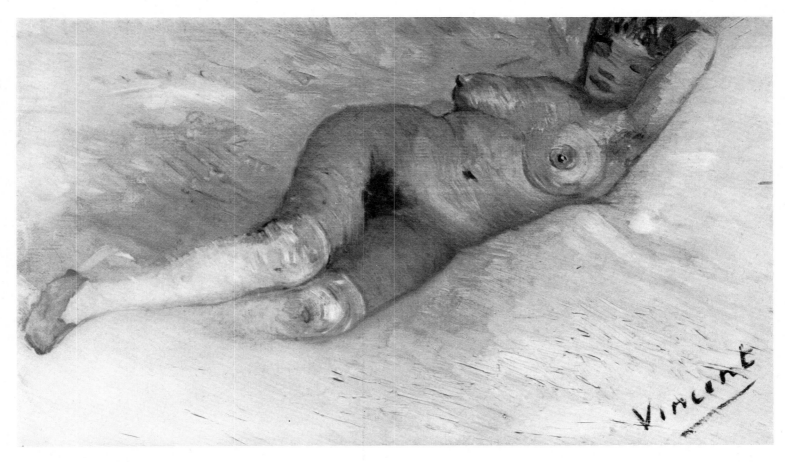

11 Reclining Nude, 1886-88.
Collection S. van Deventer, Wassenaar.

one else had. Theo had the further embarrassment that others resented what Vincent had done on Theo's account. He was no longer supporting a penniless older brother who wished to study art, but a family of four. To be sure Vincent practiced the most stringent economy. All the same necessities mounted up. Vincent had come to think of 100 francs a month as his due. Under pressure his claim rose to 150 francs, which now became his basic allowance.

Vincent met with complete ostracism, needless to say. He accepted this, yet two rejections cut him to the quick. He had counted on the painter Anton Mauve. They did not quarrel because of Christine alone. It was inevitable—Vincent resented Mauve's tutelage and Mauve resented Vincent's pretensions to ability. Then there was Tersteeg, the manager of the Goupil branch, whom Vincent had known intimately. Tersteeg was shocked, and Vincent was bitter.

The months went by, Christine's pregnancy advanced, and Vincent comforted himself with their snug domestic arrangements, the orderliness, the self-sufficiency within doors; whatever Christine lacked Vincent made up for in charity, and being conscious of his own tenderness and pity he provided his own absolution as he went along. Between whiles,

he meditated on marrying Sien, and discussed it with Theo, or rather threatened Theo with it. "If I do not marry her it would have been kinder of me to have let her alone. But by this step a chasm will be made, I decidedly 'lower' myself, as they call it, but that is not forbidden, that is not wrong, though the world calls it so. I live as a laborer. That suits me, I wanted to do so before, but could not then carry it out. I hope that across that chasm you will continue to stretch out your hand to me . . . Acquainted with the prejudices of the world, I know that what I have to do is to retire from the sphere of my own class, which anyhow cast me out long ago."

Nevertheless he listened to Theo. The marriage, apparently decided upon, was deferred until after Christine's return from the hospital. Vincent felt that he was as good as married, and he agreed to postpone the ceremony until he was earning 150 francs a month, thus balancing his obligation to Theo against his obligation to Christine. This of course was a condition which was never fulfilled, and in the end the marriage failed to take place.

Vincent moved into the house next door against Sien's return from the hospital with the baby, and exhausted himself in enthusiastic preparation, for he too had been ill. He set everything in the most

25

VI Van Gogh's Bedroom at Arles, October 1888.
Collection V. W. Van Gogh, Laren.

cheerful light and persuaded his father to come in the hope that the spectacle of mother and child would soften the old man. Theo also witnessed this idyll. He was free of his father's compunctions, but he looked on with misgiving.

Yet it must be admitted that the year and a half with Sien deepened and strengthened Vincent. He faced more than he ever had faced before. And he became an artist, painfully crossing the boundary from amateur efforts to self-confident accomplishment. He had, he wrote, "no mysterious studio, but ... *a studio with a cradle*," and it was quite natural that he found himself quoting his revered Millet: "It has always seemed to me that suicide was the deed of a dishonest man."

If the relationship was ill starred, it was not for lack of charity and devotion on Vincent's part. Vincent was, of course, offering Sien less of himself

as time went on. Or rather he was becoming his new self—in his drawing and in his painting she had a rival with which she could not compete.

That first summer, while Sien was getting back her strength, and Vincent was recovering from his own illness, he made tentative essays in oil. There were qualms—followed quickly by justifications—because of the increased expense. He clung religiously to the discipline of drawing—but still he painted. He began to discover the resources, the possibilities of the medium. But above all he discovered the joy of paint.

His thoughts on painting were sound and sane, and his taste grew stronger, more concerned with performance and less with theme. "This is, I believe, a practical palette with healthy colors," he was able to write. Finally there was a cry: "It is the painting that makes me feel so happy these days."

26

12 Père Tanguy, 1886–88.
Collection Wildenstein Galleries, New York.

And: "I know for sure that I have an instinct for color, and that it will come to me more and more, that painting is the very bone and marrow of me."

A drawing made that autumn, "Old Man with Bowed Head" (fig. 2) already had the qualities of painting. Vincent's emotional concentration was already here—even to the vortex composition. Vincent had entered into his subject by way of reverence. He was to use this drawing as a study for a painting, "On the Threshold of Eternity," when he was in the asylum at St. Rémy.

On her side, Sien recovered and became herself again, the person circumstances had made her. When Theo came the following summer the sight Vincent had to show him was woefully changed.

The house was a sty. Vincent was endeavoring to look out for the child whom he adored. Sien preferred to Vincent's poverty the ways and means she had known before, and largely upon the advice of her relations she was making excursions back into prostitution. Vincent faced up to his situation, broke up his temporary home by recognizing that it had ceased to exist, and went away. It was a painful, harrowing moment, when he turned his back on the children—such a child himself—and left Sien with moral adjurations which were neither wanted nor understood.

He needed to escape from The Hague and he went to Drenthe in the north of Holland, where his friend van Rappard had been that summer. The

27

13 Bridge at Arles, 1888.
Kröller-Müller State Museum, Otterlo.

place would have been ideal in August but now it was September and the fellow artists he had hoped to find were gone. He held on here until December, but the darkening weather, the solitude, and perhaps blind regret, gnawed into him. He sank deeper into melancholy; he feared for his health; and in short— he returned home to his parents.

IV.

His family had moved. His father had accepted a call to minister in Nuenen, a village near Eindhoven. Vincent found the new vicarage, the new territory, a refreshing experience. He prolonged his stay—

two years were to pass before he left again. Living at home, he climbed out of his small debts. His family fixed up a room in which he could paint. He took up where he left off: he was back in Brabant drawing and painting the peasant types. His parents were elderly. They now had a new community to win, and this was their final venture together. The return of the prodigal was an ordeal, painful and inescapable. At best their son was conspicuous, with his peasant appearance, his unaccountable occupation. And how long, they wondered, would he be at his best? He had squandered their good name. They were too obviously cautious. "They feel the same dread about taking me in the house," wrote Vincent,

28

14 Boats at Saintes-Maries, June 1888.
Collection V. W. Van Gogh, Laren.

"as they would about taking a big rough dog. He would run into the room with wet paws—and he is so rough. He will be in everybody's way. *And he barks so loud.* In short, he is a dirty beast... And then—the dog might bite—he might go mad, and the constable would have to shoot him."

Yet there was an incident which drew the family together. Vincent's mother hurt her leg, perhaps fractured her hip, descending from a railway carriage. Vincent at once became her nurse. Seizing on this beneficent role he found himself at the center of the family, and hence no longer eccentric. Besides, he was hard at work with charcoal and brush. He was gaining in confidence as an artist, and as his expectations grew his demands on his dealer brother grew in proportion. Was Theo really encouraging him, or was he putting him off?

When would Theo begin to sell? "... I think it is true what you say, that my work must become better still, but at the same time ... your energy to sell ... for me must become somewhat firmer too."

Living at home, his need for funds was less crying, and yet somehow Vincent and Theo managed so that the clamor for money was never stilled. Theo's contribution was now meager. Theo had his business troubles, his ups and downs; yet more than that, there was a need of tension between the two brothers which called for a continuous expression of emotional antitheses: gratitude and resentment, reproaches and forgiveness, anguish and love. Vincent's pride now required that Theo "buy" his work, a fiction which expunged the humiliation of living on an allowance. This arrangement was to

29

15 La Mousmé, July 1888.
National Gallery of Art, Collection Chester Dale, Washington, D.C.

hold for life, so that what Vincent painted was automatically Theo's: they produced it together, as Vincent often maintained. Vincent ceased in his own mind to be a protégé. There was nothing he would not give Theo and nothing he did not demand.

Yet how could Theo give Vincent a complete life, ready made? "A *wife* you cannot give me, a *child* you cannot give me, work you cannot give me. Money, yes. But of what good is it to me if I must do without the rest . . ."

This was during the winter, always a depressed season for Vincent. He grew more cheerful toward spring. The sun had an almost pagan significance for him, and it was destined to become a mighty

symbol in the disordered days ahead. His work now went on apace, and he moved his studio out of the house into the house of the sexton of the Catholic church. Whatever this meant to his parents, he felt freer. He found interesting models among the peasants, and he painted a series of weavers (fig. 3) with forthright vigor. The painting was wooden, structural, gnarled, like the subjects it described.

Vincent made friends—an odd assortment enough, hardly consonant with his father's function in the village. Above all he made the acquaintance of a lady who lived next door. The outcome of this acquaintance was not altogether Vincent's fault. The lady was the youngest of three sisters, but she

30

VII L'Arlésienne, November 1888.
Collection Sam A. Lewisohn, New York.

was far from young. She and Vincent took long summer walks together—they visited the sick. She entered Vincent's conscience rather than his heart, for his passion from now on went into his frenetic work. It was the lady who loved with belated desperation. "I too have loved at last," are the only direct words of hers which we know. Vincent remarked that he could easily have possessed her, but he refrained. Her relations rose up, with the brutality of embarrassment, to put a stop to this autumnal vagary in her existence.

Should he marry her? How to decide? "It is a pity I did not meet her *before*, for instance, ten years ago. Now she gives me the impression of a Cremona violin which has been spoiled by bad,

bungling repairers." The unfortunate woman took strichnine, and collapsed in the course of one of their walks—yet she recovered. Her family spirited her away to Utrecht. Vincent was shaken profoundly. So too was the community, and the neighbors carefully avoided the vicarage. Vincent's wretched parents were now living in isolation.

He could not bear to find himself on the losing end of a moral battle. ". . . the present Christianity I know but too well. That icy coldness bewitched even me in my youth, but I take my revenge since, how? by worshipping the love which they, the theologians, call *sin*, by respecting a whore, etc., and *not* respecting many would-be respectable, pious ladies." Beneath this bombast lay fear, the

31

fear of spiritual frost-bite; and without loving the poor woman whose existence had been blighted he seemed to take her as a sort of warning or object lesson. A painter above all must be neither meek nor subdued. "You do not know how paralyzing it is, that staring of a blank canvas ... Many painters are afraid of the blank canvas, but the blank canvas is afraid of the real passionate painter, who dares—and who has once for all broken that spell of 'you cannot.'" In theory—as well as in fact—Vincent was able to throw into his art the energies which were blocked in their normal course.

He made studies of weavers, studies of peat-diggers, and of peasants in their cottages and in the fields (fig. 4). Action, sympathy, a treatment as direct and work-a-day as his model's employment—"Peasant Woman Binding a Sheaf" was typical. His room at the sexton's was a magpie clutter of oddments, of birds' nests brought in from the heath, of brushes, paints, and tacked-up canvas; out of the snug companionship of peasants in their dim-lit huts he was building up some sort of context, some definition of himself. But if this was the rind, there was a core of aesthetic awareness; it was amazing how conscious he was of the world of art, how much got through to him, although he saw no painter but van Rappard. It all came through Theo, through letters, and the periodicals which Theo sent and Vincent devoured. He had heard of what went on in America. He knew of such names as Edwin A. Abbey and Howard Pyle.

"He seems to become more and more estranged from us," wrote his father sadly. Toward the end of March—it was 1885, Vincent's second March at home—his father suddenly fell dead on his own threshold. The uneasy balance within the family was now broken and Vincent moved out of the vicarage, unable to live with his mother alone.

Again his ambitions crowded Theo, who suggested defensively that a painting might be sent to the salon. This was a counter-challenge, and Vincent realized that he had no paintings, only studies. A canvas was needed to draw together all the studies of the winter past. Peasants around a dish of potatoes (fig. 5)—"Not always literally exact, rather never exact, for one sees nature through one's own temperament."

Aware that something had been accomplished, he shared the credit with Theo. "I repeat, let us paint as much as we can and be productive, *and be ourselves with all our faults and qualities; I say us,* because the money from you, which I know costs you trouble enough to procure me, gives you the right, when there is some good in my work, to consider half of it your own creation."

"The Potato Eaters" had been worked over more than once. The peasants' heads were "the color of a good dusty potato." Vincent feared that he might retouch and spoil the canvas. It was boxed and sent to Theo. And what did Theo think of it? He was lukewarm, apparently. The heads, built up from studies, were well enough, but the figures were less satisfactory. Theo was measuring the painting with the yardstick of Paris.

"It has not been in vain that I spent so many evenings with the miners, and peat-diggers and weavers, and peasants, musing by the fire ..." Vincent, fortified with achievement, took Theo on in endless argument. "To be perfumed is not what a peasant picture needs." Always he needed a moral stand. He pointed to Rembrandt, and warned that in future his paintings would be darker still. Theo was apparently trying to lift the key in Vincent's painting, trying to lift him out of the suppressed blacks and browns, hinting that there were new interests abroad, that the admiration for Millet was subsiding. And who, Vincent asked, were the Impressionists? Mostly by indirection, letting books speak for him, Theo ventilated his brother's tastes.

Through Theo, Vincent now came to know the writing of the Goncourt brothers; their books caught his imagination, doubtless because here were two other brothers working together. Through the Goncourts Vincent came in contact with the current taste for the Japanese. Here was something at variance with all that he had proclaimed. And yet he accepted. He was restless. He went to Amsterdam to see the museum and steeped himself in the work of Frans Hals. "At present," he wrote, "I like nothing better than to work with the brush, to draw with it too—instead of making a sketch in charcoal." And he had learned the exhilaration of speed.

Difficulties again: he had incurred the disapproval of the parish priest, who forbade posing for him. A sense that a chapter was over: his mother would now have to move from the vicarage. Vincent felt that he must get back into the world—but what world? That pull and push between the brothers was drawing him toward Paris yet holding him off. He settled for Antwerp. When he moved, he left in his studio whatever works had not been shipped to Theo. And these drawings and paintings were destined to be lost forever.

He was in Antwerp for a quarter of a year, from the end of November—the year was 1885—until the end of February. Short of money as he was, he saw the raw brutal side of the great port. He ranged the waterfront and visited the sailors' dance halls. The pressure of humanity keyed him up. Yet it was not his temperament to pursue the

16 Peasant of the Camargue, pen drawing, August 1888.
Fogg Museum of Art, Cambridge.

morbid; rather he medicined his health with the health of others, and he saw the vigor of life and not its viciousness. He saw too the marvelous health of Rubens' painting. "I am fairly carried away by his way of drawing the lines in a face with dashes of pure red ... I like Rubens just for his open-hearted way of painting, his working with the most simple means."

But Rubens was not all. Everything pressed upon him. The Goncourts had praised Japanese effects, and the docks, for Vincent, became Japanese. "My studio is not bad, especially as I have pinned a lot of little Japanese pictures on the wall..."

He spent everything on models, and Antwerp cost more than Nuenen. Yet at Nuenen he had been living in the main on black bread. Rarely or never did he have a hot meal and he grew quite giddy from lack of food. Why could not Theo send a little more money? If Theo had to chose between his brother and his creditors, why must he give to his creditors? Vincent, struggling to support himself, left his work with such dealers as he found in the city—not without qualms that this was disloyal to Theo. He had a pitiable fancy that he could succeed in painting portraits. Of whom? Well, of prostitutes, and he once suggested to the assistant of a photographer that he might procure clients. Vincent reflected that a little respectability might help here—perhaps better clothes. And above all, he decided in alarm, perhaps he needed better

33

health. He had long neglected his teeth and he had them looked to—sawed off, he related, with a loss of ten.

To avoid the cost of models he now went to an art school. Quarrels: in Vincent's view the professors were jealous of his impact on the students. Yet to some extent he submitted and humbly agreed when he was told that he needed years of practice. How was he to manage these years of further schooling and how could Theo pay—Theo who was having difficulties—unless the two brothers lived together? He must go join Theo in Paris.

Theo was uncertain, procrastinated, suggested that Vincent wait until June when they might move to a larger apartment. He suggested too that Vincent might well go back to Nuenen and help their mother, who was about to move to Breda. This was intolerable to Vincent: he was fleeing from what was left of his home *toward* Theo, and he could not turn back. He had a childlike, passionate insistence on the here and now. Theo was only putting him off.

Perhaps it was true: Theo's temperament lacked the strength for the double burden. Yet this burden was inescapable. Vincent had so woven himself into Theo's life that Theo had no existence without him. We will get another apartment in June, Theo promised, only to have a note brought to him in the gallery by a porter. "Do not be cross with me for having come all at once," was scrawled in crayon. Vincent was already in the city, he was at the Louvre, waiting for his brother in the Salon Carré. Even in this note there was the guilty word *expense*. "It comes to the same thing. We shall fix things up, you will see . . ."

V.

Theo met Vincent in the Louvre and took him home. Vincent had this way of shedding his property, of beginning each new phase of his life as though he had died and been born again. He had little to leave behind in Antwerp except his paintings; they were abandoned like his studies at Nuenen, and they too have left no trace.

There was no room for Vincent to paint in Theo's apartment and he repaired to the studio, or school, of the painter Cormon. Here, as in the school at Antwerp, he was spared the expense of private models. And he was still imbued with the idea, forced upon him in Antwerp, that he needed the long discipline of drawing from casts. He sat down before the dull plaster and struggled with agonizing perseverance to capture the delimiting line. As for the instruction at the school—again he rejected it. The important thing he gained at Cormon's was companionship.

Here he met the slight and youthful Emile Bernard, who was to become one of his very few real friends, the recipient of scores of letters after Vincent had left Paris. And he came to know a demoniac, disquieting figure, a bearded dwarf, son of a noble family from the South, a dissipated night-time creature, all sporting waistcoat, whose stunted legs made straight for the most ignoble haunts: Toulouse Lautrec.

Here suddenly was the world toward which he had so long striven, the very paint alight, aglitter, and agitated, as though with the shimmer of the ideas which took the place of paint after dark. He began to realize what Theo had meant, what Theo was trying to tell him all along, when he, Vincent was defending his blacks and browns and promising still darker pictures. Good Lord, when he was at The Hague—with Sien—he had gone to the expense of shuttering the windows, to recapture the Rembrandtesque glimmer of a dim past.

Brilliance, agitation, the quiver of life and light, this was the Impressionism of which Theo had written. And as for discussion—Vincent had always defended his ideas. If he began by listening, knowing himself for a barbaric figure, an outlander, he soon saw that others dressed like workers and starved like painters, others renounced the world and groped their way painfully forward. Vincent was not a listener for long.

During that spring of 1886 Theo was delighted with Vincent's development. "You would not recognize him, he is so much changed." The change was moral, of course, but Vincent had blossomed physically. And he had had an operation on his jaws, clearing up the rough work done on his teeth in Antwerp. We hear that he was in good spirits, and—it was well worthy of comment— "many people like him." The cautious Theo was able to say: "If we continue to live together like this, I think the most difficult period is past, and he will find his way."

By June, Theo had found a larger apartment and they moved up to Montmartre, 54 rue Lépic. The living room was snug with a stove—both brothers were sensitive to cold—and there was an all-important extra room which served as a studio so that Vincent could paint at home while Theo went down into the heart of the city, to Goupil's in the Boulevard Montmartre.

Vincent could look out over the city. He painted from the window, he ventured forth and painted Montmartre, with its wide prospect from the height of the Butte (fig. 6). He painted the cafés, the familiar landmark of the old mill of la Galette. His Paris paintings were relatively gentle, tentative even. He strove to learn, overawed by the craftsmanship about him; he was content to keep pace with

17 House at Arles, September 1888.
Collection V. W. Van Gogh, Laren.

others. Impressionism was the work of no one artist; it was curiously the result of a belief which described the nature of light. Being based on a scientific belief, one could be argued into it. Vincent did as he was taught: he lifted his key and broke up his tones.

The summers were always better. There was the sun, and Vincent was less confined. In summer he painted flower pieces, full of resplendent color, canvases for which there was no precedent in his work. And he was drawn to the Seine and its bridges, that subject, literally endless, which lent itself so to the dappling and shimmering technique of the Impressionists—for an Impressionist Vincent had become (fig. 7).

"I do not think I was wrong in my 'it must be full speed ahead,' because I see 'full steam ahead' in the future, and in the present too, as far as our energy is concerned." Vincent was writing Theo who had gone to Holland, proof at least that Vincent was in a way to be left. He was reading *Bel Ami* by Maupassant; he had at least come to physical terms with existence. It was a change from the days when he was living on Montmartre with Gladwell and flinching from the books of Michelet.

But if Vincent was temporarily thriving, he was living at Theo's expense in more ways than one. At this time Theo was handling the work of the Impressionists Monet, Pissarro and Sisley, and their allies Degas and Seurat. This was a wearing and exhausting undertaking. From the public there was mockery and acrimony, from the painters there was argument and the flare-up of raw sensibilities

35

18 Night Café, September 1888.
Collection Stephen C. Clark, New York.

characteristic of men of talent and men of ideas. From the conservative firm of Goupil there was less than tolerance—at best a half-hearted gamble on the future. Theo was obliged to sell the popular and crass in order to show the unpopular, and he was jeered at for his pains. Physically he was frailer and more delicate than his brother; aggression was not native to him; he was subject to disorders and vague nagging ailments, twinges and headaches. When he reached home, frayed, Vincent was waiting for him with some theory or problem which had by now come to a boil.

Vincent was intent on an identification with Theo. It was too late for Vincent to be a dealer, but it was not too late for Theo to be like himself. This led to a trinity of ideas as impractical as they were persistent. Theo must give up Goupil's and go on his own, giving himself entirely to worthwhile painters; Theo must found a brotherhood or union of painters; Theo must cease to be a dealer altogether and become the artist he truly was. If Theo crawled into bed he did not escape. Vincent pulled up his chair to the bedside; and by morning his monologue had blown itself out.

Theo was suffering with him, yet he always concealed it. He concealed, too, any criticism of Vincent, or his doubts about his paintings. He realized that with Vincent there would either be grandeur or there would be nothing. He was patient. "My home life is almost unbearable," he wrote to his sister. "No one wants to come see me any more." This was as it had been in the vicarage at Nuenen. "I wish he would go and live by himself, he speaks sometimes about it, but if I were to tell him to go away it would be just one more reason for him to stay."

36

VIII Woman Rocking Cradle (La Berceuse) January-March 1889.
Museum of Fine Arts, Boston.

Like Blake, Vincent cried, "Enough, or too much." The dappled strokes of the Impressionists, the stylized and organized dots of Seurat, began to flick and dash on Vincent's canvas, to organize themselves concentrically in swirling patterns, like the iron filings which describe an electrical field of force. We see this typical aspect in the Paris "Self-Portrait" (fig. 8). Like the paint he had grown sharp and brittle; he had acquired what Paris had to offer and in appearance he had almost become Theo. No longer a peasant, he was an intransigent man of ideas.

The painting of sunflowers began in Paris and not in the South. Vincent was attracted by the sunflowers grown by concierges in their narrow courtyards (fig. 9). He now painted the first of a long series. Certain subjects seemed compulsive—another persistent subject was shoes.

If the sunflowers with their warmth and color were a subject for the future, shoes, worn and battered and rendered in blacks and browns, were a subject from the past, as though they had come from Holland with him. "Three Pairs of Shoes" (fig. 10) is typical. The shoes were broken, a sole turned up

37

to show it was worn through. Here almost for the last time was his dark suppressed vision, telling us what he had left and not what he had found.

By contrast, Paris and the studio required a studio piece, the "Reclining Nude" (fig. 11). There were several such studies. No Phryne, the model was worn down by the pavements of Paris as the shoes, and her modesty was her anonymity.

There seemed to be a two-year cycle in Vincent's life; in the second year there was more difficulty, more disorder in his existence, more expression in his paint. Vincent ran into some little difficulty in this second summer in Paris. To be sure it was only with a café. The Café Tambourin was a haunt of artists, friends of Vincent's, who put up their paintings on the walls. Vincent had painted some decorations for the place and he had loaned canvases. He had tossed away a receipt, and when the café went bankrupt he ran into trouble repossessing his property. The woman who presided at the place, a former model of Gérome's, La Segattori, had trouble with Vincent and he with her. She had to warn him to go away. In a café there may be noise but not trouble. Yet on this occasion Vincent was at pains to prove that he was reasonable and not really quarrelsome, whatever his reputation. He cut himself off from the Tambourin and never went near the place again.

Was he gainer or loser in the painter acquaintances he had discovered, either at the Tambourin or in his brother's gallery or at the paint shop of an old man named Père Tanguy? In the group of artists there was a self-conscious saturnine man, cool and contemptuous, with an air of discarded elegance: Paul Gauguin. A man of genius who had thrown away his money, family and compunctions. There was something hypnotic about him. It might have been better for Vincent if they had not met.

The second winter came on and it meant painting indoors. For Vincent, this meant portraits, often self-portraits, for he would inevitably find himself alone long hours in his studio. Then the tension in him began to build up and he would out-glare himself in the mirror. From this winter dates the *Portrait of the Artist with Easel* (plate II), a solid mature work, with Impressionist means used to more sculptural ends, the strokes all weaving in the direction of the form.

Oppressed by the gray weather, he once more contemplated a move, an escape. The excitement of Paris had become turmoil merely, noise jarred on him now that it was merely noise, and motion became confusion since it lacked purpose. Gauguin had his dream of the tropics. Was it Toulouse Lautrec who suggested the south of France? Vincent was drinking too much—at least too much for his temperament. His stomach was out of order.

The truth was that he had an iron constitution, but it vibrated from the tension under which he lived.

In the midst of this drabness within and without something resplendent happened in paint, a portrait that was more Frans Hals than Impressionism, that was keyed to the gay and vivid Japanese prints tossed into its background—the portrait of Père Tanguy (fig. 12). Tanguy, the color merchant, possessed a Dickensian larger-than-life gusto, and a self-forgetful generosity. He was a Breton who had somehow become enmeshed in the Commune, the populist revolt which followed the collapse of the empire of Napoleon III, and he had served time in prison for his pains. If that were not enough he had an instinct for poverty and a fiend of a wife. She had a practical complaint; he gave away paints or took worthless canvases in trade and stuck them in his shop window. It was at Père Tanguy's that Vincent first saw the work of Cézanne on view.

For a while longer Vincent could still fancy that he was an Impressionist. But as it turned out Impressionism was only a transition, a sort of funicular which carried him to a greater height and purer light. Yet it was not light he was seeking but people and things, objects of love, and he now worked with an enveloping constructive stroke, creating rather than describing. Père Tanguy was a man he could admire, a man who had done him kindnesses, and perhaps the very title *Père* unlocked something for Vincent. It is one of the mysteries of genius—of creation, for that matter—that it can transform suffering into happiness. This alchemy had begun to work in the portrait of Père Tanguy.

VI.

Once more Vincent broke the context of his existence. He escaped to the South; he arrived in Arles late in February 1888. His life had two years to run and he was just coming into maturity as a painter. From now on the pace of his existence accelerated furiously for him and a month must be reckoned as a year. A transformation occurred, as of a chrysalis breaking. He was granted a new and dazzling, if temporary, freedom and velocity. But like those late unimaginable transformations of insects, this was a phase in which he could no longer nourish himself, in which he could only complete a function and die.

It is only rarely that we are forced to think of men's deaths in connection with their lives. It is usually the lives of saints that are prescient of their close. But this was in the character of the life of van Gogh; tragedy was part of the design, and the final

19 Outdoor Café at Night, September 1888.
Kröller-Müller State Museum, Otterlo.

Golgotha informed every preceding incident. The conclusion of his life cannot be viewed as an accident, or dismissed. Tragedy gave happiness meaning, transformed the pathetic, the ridiculous, the inept. Even the irrational became a foil to the rational and gave his thoughts power and dignity as it made his reason precious.

When Vincent arrived in Arles the city was under snow. His first impression, and it was to recur again and again, was that he had moved to Japan—to a Japan which he knew only through its colorful prints. The ruins of the Roman city, the depth of history, as palpable and exposed as the bleached cement-colored rock of the countryside, had no effect upon him.

He set himself up at an inn and began to explore. He was delighted with the change, content, with a backward glance, that Theo had a new roommate to take his place, a young Dutch painter. "In Paris one is always as down in the mouth as a cab horse, and if on top of that one has to stay all alone in the stable, it's too much."

It was Vincent of course who was now to be alone in his stable. Once out of Paris he began to remember the painters he knew, and he kept after Theo about his plan for a brotherhood of artists, with Theo their dealer at the head of a chain of galleries in Paris, London, The Hague—making use of the family connections with Tersteeg—and Vincent himself doing business at Marseilles. For Theo had

20 Public Gardens, September 1888.
Phillips Memorial Gallery, Washington, D.C.

almost made him fancy himself a dealer again, just as he liked to urge Theo to turn painter. And there was a certain deceptive logic behind the brotherhood idea. Vincent cited the Pre-Raphaelites; and it was a fact that the Impressionists had banded together in a hostile world, a fact too that the dealer Durand-Ruel had been able to captain such a group. But if Vincent's plan began with a logic which could be shared, it ended with an emotion which could not.

A brotherhood in the South would take time to develop. Meanwhile he was a painter and forerunner and he had no time to lose. By the end of February he was painting the almond blossoms, and then all the fruit trees as they came along. "I have a fresh orchard, as good as the rose-colored peach trees, apricot trees of very pale rose. At the moment I am

working on some plum trees, yellowish white, with thousands of black branches." Surely these were Japanese subjects. Impressionist subjects too, with their high key and diffuseness of form, all light and air and prismatic foam. ". . . I am actually a genuine Impressionist of the Petit Boulevard" (he still believed) "and . . . I intend to remain so." And he added, "I shall be all in when the orchards are over . . ."

The Bridge at Arles (fig. 13) was one of a series. Here he took what he wanted from Impressionism— the key, the color, the treatment of water—and went back to a solidity more native to him. The Impressionists loved streams and bridges, but so did the old Vincent from Holland, long responsive to the hypnotism of canals which flowed through the landscape mysterious yet purposeful, like green

40

IX Starry Sky, June 1889.
Museum of Modern Art, New York.

veins through flesh. And what a Japanese subject, with the angular superstructure of the drawbridge. Yet this was hardly different in composition from the weavers' looms he had painted. There was enough here for many variants. Vincent was in a literal mood of happiness and discovery.

"If I am alone—I can't help it, but honestly I have less need of company than of headlong work . . ." Still solitary, he painted all day, and at night he read. Daudet's *Tartarin de Tarascon* was his introduction to Provence. He paced the city, he sat in cafés, he grew ill at ease in his lodgings; perhaps he, the foreigner with no money, who dressed like a workman and painted in the fields—outglaring the boys who were attracted by his behavior—cut a strange figure enough. One of his climatic discoveries was the *mistral*, that fierce dry wind of Provence which tears down from the mountains to the Mediterranean: an enervating intolerable blast under a bright blue sky. Vincent learned to bury the legs of his easel deep and tie on the canvas. When he introduced little stick figures of lovers in his landscape, the man stood always wide astride as though braced before an easel. Vincent's mistress was painting itself.

His emotions were now frightfully, painfully near the surface. Something in Vincent's uncompromising nature, the same force which bungled the incidents of a normal life, made his genius more available than a man should dare to expect. His genius was becoming completely negotiable and to meet this inner inflation he was madly purchasing every experience round about him.

41

21 Iron Bridge, October 1888.
Collection Mr. and Mrs. Siegfried Kramarsky, New York.

The Vincent of a few years before was hovering around the coal pit, working in blacks and browns, shuttering down even the gray light of northern winter. Such a subdued expression might have been prolonged, kept smoldering at a low heat like the sods of his peat cutters. But there was no longer restraint in his work, only relief. What he needed, and he knew it, was companionship. For better or worse he had broken off living with Theo, and yet he was in vague search of a brother partnership. He had never graduated from a need of family life as he had known it as a child.

He longed for more pleasant quarters, a home, a studio, shelter; some physical symbol of security, and by May he had found what he wanted, a small yellow house in the Place Lamartine. Four rooms for rent in the right wing with white walls and red tile floors: Vincent could not resist it, and he took the place for fifteen months. No more living in lodgings and cafés; basically, as he wrote Theo, it was an economy. Only—the place was unfurnished. Nothing was as cheap as he fancied, and months of shopping and dickering ensued. In the end he got what he wanted. Theo put at his brother's disposal a small legacy he had just received. Vincent was able to indulge his fancy, to furnish and decorate the place. As a final luxury he even framed a few pictures. He could not bear to admit that this was just for himself. It was for Theo, a home in the country, it would be a center for the brotherhood, it was at least for a fellow painter who would live with him. He planned his own bedroom austerely enough. "For the visitor there will be the prettier room upstairs, which I shall try to

22 L'Arlésienne, Gauguin drawing, 1888.
Collection E. Hanley, Bradford, Pennsylvania.

make as much as possible like the boudoir of a really artistic woman."

And who was to join him? The logical man was Gauguin. Theo was handling Gauguin's paintings. Gauguin was ill in Brittany. He had no money, but he could pay Theo with canvases. Why should they both moulder in inns, when they might have a real home, cook their own meals, and live for next to nothing? This was the project which must have wearied Theo, yet it was true that Vincent was making heavy weather of living alone.

The negotiations which brought Gauguin to Arles took months. In the beginning Vincent passed on to Theo much shrewd comment on the agonized self-pitying letters from Gauguin. Vincent saw Gauguin quite as he was until his own emotions became too involved. But it was a long time before the moody Gauguin capitulated, and by then Vincent's expectations had built up to a pitch which could have no sequel but disappointment and despair.

The preparation for an easier life in the Place Lamartine was for months only an added strain; the change conceived as an economy required a capital outlay; there were unforseen necessities such as putting in gas. When Vincent came to move he had a quarrel with his landlord who had raised his board; apparently the additional charge turned on no more than a better quality of wine from a time when Vincent's stomach was upset. But

43

X Olive Trees, 1889.
Minneapolis Institute of Arts.

it meants going before a judge, since Vincent made it a principle not to yield. He came off rather better than he had hoped, but he was battered by the experience.

All this time Vincent was painting at a fever pitch. The pending move was not allowed to slow the work. He wished to have as much done as possible by the time Gauguin arrived. He was hoping to profit from Gauguin, but he wanted to show him that he had some ability of his own. This was the season of daily masterpieces, of day-long work or night-long work followed by exhausted sleep.

He could hardly be so near to the Mediterranean and not see it, and by June he had made a trip to a little fishing village which caught for the Marseilles market. Here he made drawings which turned into paintings: "Boats at Saintes-Maries" (fig. 14). The little boats, already in primary colors, reminded him of so many flowers. They were like insects too, with sensitive antenae. They lent themselves to the bright flat patterns of the Japanese print.

He struck up an acquaintance with a Zouave whom he painted in all his innocent flamboyance. "And now, if you know what a 'mousmé' is, I have just painted one . . . (fig. 15). A mousmé is a Japanese girl—Provençal in this case—12 to 14 years old. That makes two portraits now, the Zouave and herself." A literal, disarming, careful painting. For some reason his attack was more cautious. Was it tenderness for his model that slowed his brush? The painting took him all of a week.

Besides the young and easygoing Zouave, Vincent fell in with someone else he could talk to, a young New England watercolorist, Dodge McKnight.

44

There was no argument in McKnight. Silent by nature, he made no rejoinders. He said little about Vincent's work, and Vincent did not conceal his opinion of McKnight's. They saw each other from time to time, but there was no bond between them. Real friendship, a genuine and lasting response, was to develop in a more unlikely quarter. He grew intimate with the postman Roulin and his wife, and out of this pair he improvised a family, making them do duty as his parents although they were hardly of an age for such a role. Yet they played the part. This was one of the very few friendships of Vincent's which survived. It began as an oddity in human relations, and rose to an act of nobility on the Roulins' part, unsullied by any awareness that their unhappy friend was a genius.

Vincent painted the Roulin family, beginning with the postman himself, first a head, then the more famous portrait (plate III) "in a blue uniform, trimmed with gold, a big bearded face, very like Socrates." It has been reproduced almost too much for its own good, yet it is still astonishing in its directness. Vincent realized that here he had Tanguy over again. "I once watched him sing the Marseillaise, and I thought I was watching '89, not next year, but that of 99 years ago. It was a Delacroix, a Daumier, straight from the old Dutch." And so for that matter was the canvas. It was Frans Hals again, and not only in the wonderful instantaneous handling, but in that pastry-colored flesh peculiar to Hals.

The same month saw the sunflower series. He had painted sunflowers the year before in Paris. Now they became a resplendent symbol, both for the gold color and perhaps because the word *sun* was caught in their name. "I am now at the fourth picture of sunflowers . . . This fourth is a bunch of 14 flowers against a yellow background, like a still life of quinces and lemons I did . . . Only as it is much bigger, it gives a rather singular effect..." (plate IV).

Well before the arrival of Gauguin, Vincent knew that the actual amount of color counted for something. "Do you remember that one day we saw at the Hotel Drouot a very extraordinary Manet, some huge pink peonies with their green leaves against a light background? As much the open air and as much a flower as anything could be . . . That is what I call simplicity of technique. And I must tell you that nowadays I am endeavoring to find a brushwork without stippling or anything else, nothing but the varied stroke. But some day you will see." So his painting was far from innocent, even if it was direct. It had also ceased to be Impressionism, and by now Vincent knew it.

He drew, and also painted, an old peasant "who has a very strong resemblance to Father in feature, only he was more ordinary and bordered on caricature. Nevertheless I should have been very keen to do him exactly the poor peasant that he was." The "Peasant of the Camargue" (fig. 16) was Patience Escalier, former cowherd. Vincent had used Impressionism to transform his painting, and then put it behind him; and the same thing was true of his drawing. Here he continued to stipple, creating almost abstract patterns with dots and brittle strokes. And by these means he captured an effect of intense light which was characteristic of his drawings made in the South.

"Ideas for my work come to me in swarms." He had yet to move to the yellow house but after all it was his, and he painted it (fig. 17) "in sulphur-colored sunshine" under a fierce cobalt sky that had none of the transparency of northern air, that was more filled with menace than hope. He attacked his total environment, the house, the café. "Night Café" (fig. 18), actually the Café de l'Alcazar in the Place Lamartine, was again a masterpiece, peculiarly Vincent's work in the expressive way everything was sacrificed to emotional purpose. "The room is blood red and dark yellow with a green billiard table in the middle; there are four lemon yellow lamps with a glow of orange and green. Everywhere there is a clash and contrast of the most alien reds and greens in the figures of the little sleeping houlligans, in the empty dreary room, in violet and blue. The blood red and the yellow green of the billiard table for instance contrast with the soft tender Louis XV green of the counter on which there is a nosegay in rose color. The white coat of the patron, on vigil in a corner of this furnace, turns lemon yellow, or pale luminous green." The ominousness, either in the paint or the words, conveys a sense of fear and guilt which is at once countered with a moral judgment and transposed into a sense of sin. "In my picture of the 'Night Café' I have tried to express the idea that the café is a place where one can ruin oneself, run mad, or commit a crime."

Vincent had freed himself from the religious compunctions of his youth, just as he had broken through the suppressed blacks and browns of his early painting. Freed himself?—in principle, but the barriers set up at the vicarage were not so easily broken down. "'Man becomes ambitious as soon as he becomes impotent,'" he recalled reading. "Now though it's pretty much all one to me whether I'm impotent or not," he commented, "I'm damned if that's going to drive me to ambition." He fell back on continence, or at least moderation, as a prescription for such a nature as his own.

Vincent was careless of his health, and when he ran out of money, as he did about every ten days,

23 L'Arlésienne, 1888.
Collection Dr. and Mrs. Harry Bakwin, New York.

his stomach was the loser. Then he lived on coffee. But he was also attentive to his symptoms, and he was attentive to Theo's symptoms too. Theo suffered from nervous exhaustion, sciatica, and other vague and general malaises, which he was quite willing to share with Vincent by mail, thus jeopardizing Vincent's security, for both brothers were dependent on Theo's salary. By keeping Vincent anxious about money, Theo kept Vincent as worried as Vincent kept him. Anxiety was the drug which they provided for each other.

Weighing the past with the present, Vincent spoke of his drinking in Paris—how he had nearly become a drunkard, whereas in Provence he was so keyed up that he grew tipsy on a glass of brandy. The latter statement is probably the clue to his condition. What was normal for an adult was dissipation for him. He even considered his constant pipe-smoking a debauch.

In September he painted another café scene, "Outdoor Café at Night" (fig. 19) "with the terrace lit up by a big gas lamp in the blue night, and a corner of starry blue sky." The stars were not points, but palpable globules abloom in the night air. From now on heavenly bodies became obsessive objects for Vincent. ". . . to look at the stars always makes me dream, as simply as I dream over the black dots of a map representing towns and villages. Why, I ask myself, should the shining dots of the sky not be as accessible as the black

46

24 Portrait of the Artist with a Pipe, January-February 1889.
Collection Mr. and Mrs. Leigh B. Block, Chicago.

dots on the map of France? If we take the train to reach Tarascon or Rouen, we take death to reach a star. One thing undoubtedly true in this reasoning is this, that while we are *alive* we *cannot* get to a star, any more than when we are dead, we can take the train.

"So it seems to me that cholera, gravel, phthisis and cancer are the celestial means of locomotion, just as steamboats, omnibuses and railways are the terrestrial means. To die quietly of old age would be to go there on foot.

"This week I have done absolutely nothing but paint and sleep and take my meals. That means sittings of twelve hours, of six hours, and so on, and then a sleep of twelve hours at a time." He

was writing to Theo on the seventeenth of September. The next day he finally moved into his new house.

Two paintings of the Public Gardens approach humanity more cheerfully. The more animated and effective scene of the two (fig. 20) shows us a figure typically astride in the foreground. The walk leads the eye into quick perspective, which is so constant and restless a characteristic.

We have seen this lurching perspective, almost a camera effect, in the "Night Café." We find it again in a painting where the space is actually very confined—the "Bedroom in Arles" (plate VI) in which Vincent portrays the interior of his new house. "...here color is to do everything, and

47

giving by its simplification a grander style to things, is to be suggestive here of *rest* or of sleep in general. In a word, to look at the picture ought to rest the brain or rather the imagination.

"The walls are of pale violet. The ground is of red tiles.

"The wood of the bed and chairs is the yellow of fresh butter, the sheets and pillows very light greenish lemon.

"The coverlet scarlet. The window green.

"The toilet table orange, the basin blue.

"The doors lilac.

"And that is all—there is nothing in this room with closed shutters.

"The broad lines of the furniture again must express inviolable rest. Portraits on the wall, a mirror, and a towel and some clothes." The painting here described had yet to be done. "Tomorrow very early I am going to begin in the cool morning light . . ." There were to be several versions. Vincent still thought of most of his paintings as studies. When he worked out an arrangement which satisfied him—or nearly satisfied him—as a painting, he was quite willing to repeat it.

Happiness: "My dear Theo we are in the right way at last. Certainly it does not matter being without hearth or home so long as one is young, and living like a traveler in cafés, but it was becoming unbearable to me, and more than that it did not fit in with my thoughtful work." It is not just for themselves. "If we set up here a studio and refuge for some one or other of the crowd who is in want, no one will ever be able to reproach either you or me with living or spending for ourselves alone. . . . such a studio needs a floating capital, and I have swallowed that up during my unproductive years, but now that I am beginning to produce something, I shall pay it back.

"At present I do not think my pictures are worthy of the goodness I have had from you, but once they are worthy I swear that you will have created them as much as I, and that we are fashioning them together."

These dangerous moments of happiness and hope: "I wanted to do some more sunflowers as well, but they were already over . . . I have a terrible lucidity at moments, these days when nature is so beautiful, I am not conscious of myself any more and the picture comes to me as in a dream."

Now followed one of the great self-revelations, the "Portrait of the Artist. Dedicated to Gauguin" (plate V). Here the mark of the inner fervor or fever has set its seal upon him. "I have bought of set purpose a mirror good enough for me to be able to work from myself in default of a model, because if I can manage to paint the coloring of my own head, which is not to be done without

some difficulty, I shall likewise be able to paint the heads of other good souls, men and women."

The studio in the South; the brotherhood, Gauguin. A myth of expectation was building up. In the early days Vincent's expectations were simple. "I have been thinking about Gauguin and here it is... there is Gauguin's journey and there are two beds or two mattresses, which in that case we absolutely must buy. But afterwards, as Gauguin is a sailor, we shall probably manage to grub at home." From Gauguin himself there was not a word for over a month. "Whether Gauguin comes or not, it is his own business, and directly we are ready to have him, and his bed and room are there, we shall be keeping our promise. Well, Gauguin and I must look forward, we must contrive to have a roof over our heads, beds, the absolute necessities in short, to stand the siege of failure which will last *all our lives*, and we must settle down in the cheapest place." But Vincent's patience was running out. "Perhaps he thinks that I shall always be here and that he has our word. But it is not too late to retract it, and I really am strongly tempted to do so, because failing him, I should naturally think of another partnership . . ." But Vincent did go ahead with his preparations. "I have bought one walnut bed, and another in white wood, which will be mine . . . The room you will have then, or Gauguin, if Gauguin comes, will have white walls with a decoration of great yellow sunflowers. In the morning when you open the window, you see the green of the gardens and the rising sun, and the road into the town." In spite of all this Gauguin was uncertain, and he kept Vincent on tenter-hooks. "I think it absolutely unfair," Vincent began reasonably, "that you who have just sent money which you yourself had to borrow, for the furnishing of the house, should also have to bear the expense of the (Gauguin's) journey . . . Gauguin is married, and we must thoroughly realize in advance that in the long run it is not certain that our various interests will be compatible." But soon imagination won out over reason: "Do you realize that if we get Gauguin we are at the beginning of a very great thing, which will open a new era for us . . .? We have to add over and above all this Gauguin's fare . . . *Gauguin's fare before everything*, to the detriment of your pocket and mine. *Before everything*. All the expenses I have mentioned," Vincent confessed, "are all with the idea of making a good impression on him on his arrival . . . Gauguin and not I will be head of the studio . . ." Gauguin was, however, still ailing; or at least he was inert. "He must eat and go for walks with me in lovely surroundings, pick up a nice girl now and then, see the house as it is and as we shall make it, and altogether enjoy himself."

XI Ravine, December 1889.
Museum of Fine Arts, Boston.

The "Iron Bridge" (fig. 21) is well ahead of Vincent's time in its feeling for structure, for the tension of divergent directions, for the perspective which suggests the invisible tracks. But what concerned Vincent was doubtless the railroad itself and the expectation which went with it. "I wrote again to Gauguin the day before yesterday to say once again that he would probably recover more quickly here.

"And he will do such beautiful things here.

"He will need time to recover, I tell you."
Gauguin finally arrived—it was the twentieth of October—looked cooly over Vincent's wares, which were on display for him, and condescended to give Vincent pointers. He took the credit, later, for whatever Vincent had to offer. It was remarkable that the two men held together as long as they did.

Poverty has held many together. And then they had their expectations. Vincent hoped to help Gauguin. Gauguin hoped for help from Theo, his dealer. Gauguin sized up the situation, made the best of it, and took over. He cooked, he set things in order, he put Vincent in his place. They argued, needless to say. "Our arguments are terribly *electric*, we come out of them sometimes with our heads as exhausted as an electric battery after it is discharged." Vincent's tastes were largely moral preferences, and moral preferences disgusted Gauguin.

Vincent painted "L'Arlésienne," the café keeper, Madame Ginoux (plate VII). Once more the influence was consciously Japanese, with the brittle concave arabesque crisp against the gold ground, ". . . a figure slashed on in an hour, background

25 White Roses, May 1889.
Collection Mr. and Mrs. William Averell Harriman.

pale lemon, the face gray, the clothes black, black, black, with perfectly raw Prussian blue. She is leaning on a green table and seated in an armchair of orange wood." Along with the news of this masterpiece went word of equal importance in terms of Vincent's hopes and peace of mind: "Gauguin and I are going to have our dinner at home to-day, and we feel as sure and certain that it will turn out well as that it will seem to us better and cheaper."

Gauguin in his turn made a drawing of Madame Ginoux (fig. 22) and Vincent painted her again from Gauguin's drawing (fig. 23). The copy is very close, and yet Vincent's painting does not really resemble Gauguin's drawing. Inescapably both artists put themselves into their work. In Gauguin, Madame Ginoux is all Gauguin: cool, suave, linear

and calculating. In Vincent's copy, she is all Vincent: rough, gnarled, bewildered, pathetic.

There was something dynamic about Paul Gauguin, a vitality of another order than Vincent's, based on a denial of moral obligation. A flirtation with the diabolic, a setting of freedom and action above compunction and obligation, was part of the self-induced desolation of the romantic theme from the days of Byron. Gauguin combined this physical haughtiness with the cult of the primitive. Doubtless he was to prove something less than his claim: he was no more a stevedore than Vincent was a peasant. He too had a vigorous physique; but he succumbed to his pretensions, and shattered himself in the course of time.

Yet Gauguin seems to have been reasonable and orderly at Arles, with a rational if burly balance

50

26 Cornfield with Reaper, June 1889.
Kröller-Müller State Museum, Otterlo.

between work, alcohol, and the ever convenient brothel down the street. But his way of living was enough to upset the delicate balance or imbalance of Vincent's childlike existence. Vincent was faced with Gauguin's instigation to manhood and implied contempt. Something in the situation was too much for him. The storm broke on Christmas Eve.

Two other disturbing factors may have weighted the scales against Vincent. Madame Roulin had had another child during the autumn, and Vincent was painting her rocking a cradle (plate VIII). This subject obsessed him and there were to be six variants altogether. A child in a cradle—that was the living scene Vincent showed his father in the studio in The Hague. When he was decorating his house in Arles, "I am going to paint my own

bed," he wrote. "There will be three subjects on it. Perhaps a nude woman, I have not decided, perhaps a child in a cradle, I do not know, but I shall take my time over it." In the painting of Madame Roulin one saw neither child nor cradle, one simply looked up at the woman. Vincent actually intended the painting as a decoration for the house, to be placed between sunflowers. But the painting was broken off for the time being—the crisis intervened.

However much or little the cradle theme may have unsettled Vincent, it was only on the surface—literally on canvas—and it could be set aside. But there was something else, a totally new and unknown factor in Vincent's life which could not be escaped. Nor could Vincent even admit that it was a threat. Theo was about to marry. In fact, he was marrying

51

XII Houses at Auvers, June-July 1890.
Museum of Fine Arts, Boston.

27 Grove of Cypresses, pen, pencil and wash, June 1889.
Art Institute of Chicago.

over the Christmas holidays. Would there still be sustenance and love—would Theo's wife be another sister or a rival? What would become of this intense brotherhood with Theo? Gauguin was no substitute for Theo; he was not the brother on whom Vincent relied.

The outcome is too well known; Vincent made attacks of progressive seriousness on Gauguin. Doubtless they began as incitements to counter attack: "A few times during the night he got up and came near my bed," wrote Gauguin. "'What made you wake up,' he asked me. 'What is the matter with you,' I said. Without answering he went back to bed and slept like a log." Then one evening at the café, Vincent—who had had an absinthe—threw his glass in Gauguin's face. "I took him in my arms, and after crossing the square, Vincent went to bed where he fell asleep almost immediately." Whatever the impulsive act which Vincent was blotting out in sleep, it is understandable that Gauguin prepared to beat a retreat. But this threat of desertion was too much for Vincent. As Gauguin was loitering in the open toward the close of the day Vincent came rushing after him armed with a razor, flinched at his own intention, and ran home.

Vincent now turned his violence back on himself, cut off a portion of his ear and took it to a woman in a brothel. At this turn of events Gauguin telegraphed Theo. It was that season when Vincent

53

turned toward home regardless—Christmas Eve. The telegram brought Theo on Christmas Day. Out of agony and love Vincent had succeeded in postponing his brother's wedding.

Theo found Vincent in evil case. There had been public excitement. The good Roulin had taken Vincent home. A crowd had intruded. The police intervened. Vincent had lost much blood, became unconscious, and was taken to the hospital.

After a few days of crisis Vincent recovered and Theo went back to Paris accompanied by Gauguin, who was only too glad to explain himself away and attach himself to his dealer. In the hospital at Arles, Vincent was in charge of a Doctor Rey. A Protestant minister, the Reverend Doctor Salles, also concerned himself with Vincent; and Roulin did not forsake him.

Vincent was sane, but he was subject to seizures. During his lifetime his disturbance was thought to be epilepsy. He had no recollection of his seizures—he only knew that he suffered intensely. He had hallucinations which turned on religious themes. Long before he had written Theo: "I do not think that my madness could take the form of persecution, since my feelings when in a state of excitement lead me rather to the consideration of eternity, and eternal life."

VII

The transition from Arles to the asylum at St. Remy took a quarter of a year. Vincent recovered quickly from his crisis and was soon out of the hospital. He even made light of the whole matter, spoke of the needlessness of Theo's coming, and blamed Gauguin for sending for him. He was able to face himself wearing the bandage of his mutilation (fig. 24) and painted himself quietly smoking his pipe. He painted Gauguin's empty chair. And he finished the canvas which had been so agonizingly broken off, for which Madame Roulin had posed. He had painted two other variants of it by the end of the month. Madame Roulin was given her choice, and Vincent painted the fourth variant, the one reproduced.

"I have a canvas of the "Woman Rocking a Cradle," the very one I was working on when my illness interrupted me. I have two copies now of that as well.

"I have just been saying to Gauguin about this picture that when he and I were talking about the Icelandic fishermen and of their mournful isolation, exposed to all dangers, alone on the sad sea, I have just been saying to Gauguin, that following those intimate talks of ours, the idea came to me to paint such a picture, that sailors, who are at once children and martyrs, seeing it in the cabin of their boat should feel the old sense of cradling come over them and remember their own lullabys."

If by the sailor he meant Gauguin, it was Vincent who was both child and martyr. For the moment he had recovered, but life could hardly be expected to be easier. The owner of the yellow house, for instance, had arranged during Vincent's absence to turn him out in favor of a new tenant. This was blocked for the time being. But the recent upheaval had been expensive and the problem of money was once more acute. Vincent had some thought that his support might come to him through Theo's new wife. "Let it go to your wife's hands, who will join with us besides in working with the artists." "Meantime this tender-hearted wife of yours will have come, and will make us old fellows almost young again."

As for his health, "The unbearable hallucinations have ceased," and again, ". . . I am amazed to be getting better." Yet he took a subdued view of his condition and with reason: "As for considering myself as altogether sane, we must not do it."

In February he had to be confined again. This time when he emerged he was confronted with a petition for his incarceration which had been circulated through the neighborhood. The Reverend Dr. Salles tried to find a place for Vincent elsewhere in Arles; but this was too much of a challenge. Vincent came to approach, voluntarily, his own hospitalization as the lesser of two evils. "The thing is to swallow the real facts of your destiny, and then there you are." He was forced out of his house, then went to the hospital, then—Theo was returning to Paris with his wife—Vincent accepted the arrangements which took him to St. Rémy.

"To begin again that painter's life from now on, isolated in the studio so often, and without any other means of distraction than going to a café or a restaurant with all the neighbors criticizing, etc., *I can't face it:* to go and live with another person, say another artist—difficult, very difficult—it's taking too much responsibility on one's self. I dare not even think of it."

The asylum of St. Paul de Mandole was a large eighteenth-century building with a courtyard, ample rooms and monotonous corridors. Here Vincent was given two rooms overlooking the garden. In the distance—between the bars—he could see the low brown Alps. Doctor Peyron, the superintendent, allowed Vincent special privileges. Wisely, mercifully, he was permitted to paint, and naturally he did the view from his window, and then the garden. Soon he was allowed to go out into the fields and hills. Eventually he was even allowed to go (attended) to Arles.

54

28 Road with Cypresses, May 1890.
Kröller-Müller State Museum, Otterlo.

Under the quiet regime his health greatly improved, yet his seizures recurred, and they struck with little or no warning. Their return was all the more horrifying in that between whiles he was sane. Living with the insane was the penalty he had to pay.

The stridency which had always characterized him now appeared to be concentrated into these spells of hysteria. If anything he was now more sane at other times. Calmness of spirit had been urged upon him; but since it was his nature or genius to transform all mundane experience, his calmness became almost serenity under inconceivable circumstances: his martyrdom had its spiritual grace. He wrote to Theo, he read and he painted; his life was not so different after all. His letters became sporadic and on occasion confused, but his work continued at the same pace. From May to September—he was to stay a year, until the following May at St. Rémy—he painted nearly one hundred and fifty pictures. This was more than a canvas a day. It meant protracted sessions before the easel, followed by intervals of heavy sleep. He no longer woke up to a world he could control; instead he created one daily. "My dear brother— it is always in between my work that I write to you—I am working like one actually possessed, more than ever I am in a dumb fury of work. And I think that this will help to cure me." Undoubtedly it helped.

55

29 Portrait of the Artist, September 1889.
Collection John Hay Whitney, New York.

"Since it is just the season when there are plenty of flowers and consequently color effects, it would perhaps be wise to send me five meters more of canvas.

"For the flowers are short lived and will be replaced by the yellow cornfields. Those especially I hope to catch better than I did at Arles. The *mistral* (since there are some mountains) seems much less tiresome than at Arles where you always got it first hand.

"When you receive the canvas that I have done in the garden, you will see that I am not too melancholy here." The superb "White Roses" (fig. 25) was painted in the month of his arrival. He painted the iris in the garden; there were many other canvases in which he entered innocently into the joy of living things.

But at St. Rémy a change came over his painting. His brush now had a wild sweep, his forms an organic flow. Tormented curves and the flickering and coiling forms of fire were omnipresent and a great low sun—he saw it rise through the bars of his window—became an obsessive symbol. As though the sun had both blessed and smitten him, he began to believe that madness was indigenous to the climate, and no wonder, since he now lived surrounded by the mad.

Forms writhed, and they fell into unconscious images of people. This had always been characteristic of his work in some degree, the human intruding

56

30 Road Menders, November 1889.
Cleveland Museum of Art.

wherever possible. Now it was exaggerated. In the "Cornfield with Reaper" (fig. 26), painted in June, the mountain outline was mysteriously a recumbent self-portrait, the headland his own head.

The cornfield, the reaper and his scythe, and then the cypress: in other words, the harvest and death. "The cypresses are always occupying my thoughts, and I would like to make something of them like the canvases of the sunflowers, because it astonishes me that they have not yet been done as I see them." The theme haunted him. "Now what the willow is at home," he was saying six months later, "that is just the significance of the olive and the cypress here." And later still, as he was almost ready to leave: "When I had done those sunflowers,

I looked for the opposite and yet the equivalent and I said—it is the cypress."

"Grove of Cypresses" (fig. 27) and "Cypresses" (plate I), both dating from this same June, show well enough the new flamelike aspect in his drawing and in his paint. The basic compositional element in these late works is the vortex, perhaps the least suppressed of all forms, the most vertiginous, the most detached from the pull of gravity. The vortex is most obvious, most free to be itself, when it is coiling around a star in Vincent's painting, hypnotically centered on an actual point of fire. The "Starry Sky" (plate IX) painted this same month, is one of the greatest of these ecstatic and vertiginous works. But all of these late paintings, taken together, are an epic whose subject is life and death, light and dark, day and night, yellow and blue, and their motion is somehow planetary—natural though not of this earth. "Starry Sky" is one of the world's last great religious paintings, and its subject is immortality.

It is time to look ahead to the latest variation on the cypress theme, "Road with Cypresses" (fig. 28), painted nearly a year later, just before Vincent left St. Rémy. Cypress and star, death and resurrection, are all too obvious, yet with Vincent they do not seem to be consciously obvious, and doubtless there lies their strength. "I have still from down there a cypress with a star, a last attempt—a night sky with a moon without radiance, the slender crescent barely emerging from the opaque shadow cast by the earth—a star with exaggerated brilliance, if you like, a soft brilliance of rose and green in the ultramarine sky across which are hurrying some clouds . . .

"On the road a yellow cart with a white horse in harness, and two late wayfarers. Very romantic, if you like, but Provence also, I think . . ." One of the late wayfarers has a shovel over his shoulder, a laborer. Are they brothers?

Next only to Vincent's interest in the cypresses was his response to the olive orchards. Vincent painted them again and again, through this first (and last) autumn. The "Olive Trees" (plate X) is the most formal and massive of the group; the mountains, and the implacable sun, set in its vortex of vibrant strokes, organize the diffuse tangle of the orchard.

There is a different pace in these paintings than in our daily lives; if we expect paintings to be inert while we are in motion, here it is the other way about, for Vincent is living more rapidly than we. The eerie, perfervid "Portrait of the Artist" (fig. 29) has an alert anxious flicker which seems to correspond not to the motion of the hand but to that of the eye, or even to the pace of thought. Cool to a subterranean degree, it was painted in the lingering heat of September.

The "Road Menders" (fig. 30), dates from November. It is full of objective structural power. But what a tormented jungle of a universe a few old trees create, and one suspects the road menders, working over their stone slabs, of being grave diggers. The "Ravine" (plate XI), painted in December—to move from masterpiece to masterpiece, for there is more and not less van Gogh out of St. Rémy—is tortuous with a sense of the difficulties ahead, yet not without hope, as though, if the water can win through, so can man. Yet the painter's own conscious mood was far from depressed. "For the moment I am working at a picture of a path between the mountains," he wrote to his mother, "and a little brook, thrusting

between the stones. The rocks are of a plain violet-gray or pink, with here and there palm bushes and a kind of broom, which through the autumn has all kinds of colors, green, yellow, red, brown. And the brook in the foreground, white and foaming like soapsuds and further on reflecting the blue of the sky."

Winter meant days indoors, even in the South. Confined to his room, Vincent took to copying, or "translating," as he called it, lifting into color the black and white works of Delacroix, Daumier and Millet, his sources the prints sent him by Theo. He had serious qualms about his right to do this. ". . . in music . . . the *interpretation* of a composer is something, and it is not a hard and fast rule that only the composer should play his own composition.

"I pose the black and white of Delacroix or Millet or something taken from them as a subject.

"And then I improvise color on it . . .

". . . my brush goes between my fingers as a bow would on the violin and absolutely for my pleasure."

In the autumn he had painted the "Pietà," after Delacroix (fig. 31), and if the figure of Christ is an unconscious self-portrait, this is understandable. Months later, in the following May, he painted "The Resurrection of Lazarus", after Rembrandt (fig. 32). Here too the portrait is his own; and in the center of the composition is the familiar great low sun. It should be obvious that this is the rising sun of the worker in the fields, and of Vincent too, who went to sleep like a child at an early hour, and rose avid for the light.

The late paintings from St. Rémy show an intensification both of hope and despair. This corresponded to Vincent's condition. In the beginning he was steeped in the apathy that came of fear. He needed his courage. "But without joking, the *fear* of madness is leaving me a good deal, as I see at close quarters those who are affected by it, as in the future I may very easily be.

"For though there are some who howl or rave continually there is much real friendship here one for another, they say, we must put up with others so that others will put up with us . . . And between ourselves we understand each other very well. I can for instance sometimes chat with one of them who can only answer in incoherent sounds, because he is not afraid of me.

"If someone has an attack the others look after him and interfere so that he does himself no harm.

"The same for those whose mania is to fly often into rages. The old inhabitants of the menagerie run up and separate the combatants, if combat there is . . ." There is no more serious threat to

31 Pietà (after Delacroix), September 1889.
Collection V. W. Van Gogh, Laren.

a man than loss of his reason, yet Vincent surmounted the threat. Pity liberated him. The mind of man is not really limited by madness, for through madness it has been understood.

As he grew better his hopes began to stir beneath his abnegation—even as in the Borinage. He was allowed trips to Arles, and the trips brought on new attacks. And then his despair was great in proportion to his hopes, which kept returning again as the intervals lengthened between attacks. He began to entertain serious thoughts of getting out, of going north, of returning to a cooler, more familiar climate. What was to be the end of all this? "What to do—to go on these months here or to move—I don't know. The point is that the

crises when they occur are no joke, and to risk having an attack like that with you or other people, is a serious business."

He found a strong argument for moving in the fact that he was in an institution maintained by the church. His seizures were replete with religious fancies which might be dispelled, he hoped, in a civic atmosphere. "When I realize that here the attacks tend to take an absurd religious turn, I should almost venture to think that this even *necessitates* my return to the north." And again, ". . . I get embroiled and (have) frightful ideas about religion such as I never had in the north."

It would not be easy to find a solution. The city of Paris was certainly not the answer. Theo was

32 Resurrection of Lazarus (after Rembrandt), May 1890.
Collection V. W. Van Gogh, Laren.

struggling to discover the right person to care for Vincent. They both thought of the elderly and benign painter Pissarro, oldest of the Impressionist group, who lived at Auvers in the country outside of Paris. And Theo knew of a Doctor Gachet, who also lived at Auvers. Gachet was a physician, semiretired, with a consulting room in Paris. He had a predilection for artists and the arts and was himself a painter and etcher. He owned paintings—he had known Cézanne, and he had even known Corot and Daumier. And so the brothers wrote back and forth about Gachet, and little by little Vincent's liberty was plotted.

There were seizures and postponements, but there was fresh expectation in Vincent's heart, and even some suspicion that Doctor Peyron might hold him back. As always, Vincent left in a rush. It was

May, the perfect season in the year to arrive in the north.

One hardly needs to account for Vincent's growing desire to leave St. Rémy. Nor can one pin motives—always so complex—on a coincidence. Yet something should be given more weight than Vincent was capable of giving it himself. Theo and his new wife Jo were having a child. Vincent's original crisis had come on with Theo's marriage, which it postponed. When the marriage was a fact Vincent withdrew to St. Rémy. All through the autumn at St. Rémy, he tenderly shared the expectation of Theo and his wife, which in Vincent was a gradual gestation of hope. After the child was born he began to think of a return to the north. Theo had named the child Vincent. It was almost as if Vincent had had to look into the cradle to make sure that this child was not himself.

60

33 Portrait of Doctor Gachet, June 1890.
Collection Mr. and Mrs. Siegfried Kramarsky, New York.

VIII.

Vincent insisted on traveling alone and arrived in Paris on the morning of May 18. Theo went to meet him, and they drove from the station in an open cab, cheerfully up familiar Montmartre to the Cité Pigalle. Vincent met his sister-in-law, Jo, and now actually saw his namesake—he did look in the cradle. Jo was struck that Vincent looked so much stronger and healthier than her husband. All went well. He saw old friends. But the first thing he discovered, of course, was his own life's work as it had accumulated in Theo's apartment.

Only one painting of Vincent's was sold during his lifetime. Theo seemed curiously reticent when it came to bringing Vincent's work forward. By now he certainly believed in it, yet he had kept it close. Nor did Vincent really wish his paintings to be dispersed. For all the clamor for sales, one cannot escape the impression that Vincent's painting, the bond between these two brothers, was too much a part of them to be sold. So here was Vincent's work from the beginning, the "Potato Eaters" over the mantle, and canvases unframed stacked under the sofa, under the bed, crowding the spare room. Vincent sat down on the floor and became reacquainted with himself.

After three happy days in Paris, Vincent was transplanted to Auvers and introduced to Dr. Gachet. Vincent found the doctor eccentric. ". . . his

34 Crows over the Wheatfields, July 1890.
Collection V. W. Van Gogh, Laren.

experience as a doctor must keep him balanced enough to combat the nervous trouble from which he certainly seems to me to suffer at least as seriously as I do." Gachet had taken a room for Vincent, but Vincent immediately gave it up in favor of a cheaper and noisier place kept by a Monsieur Ravoux, opposite the town hall.

Vincent liked Auvers at once. The thatched farm houses, the buildings with such hunched, living lines that they might have been cattle grazing by the roadside, and the sweeping fields, that seem, in France, to reach to such far horizons—he at once settled to paint. He had arrived disorganized and disturbed, and the change was complete—from confinement to liberty. Yet he hardly paused. In the next two months he completed some fifty-six canvases, and he made many drawings besides. He maintained the pace he had set himself at Arles and at St. Rémy. His balance depended on being in constant motion.

Vincent soon came to like Dr. Gachet. "The impression I got of him was not unfavorable," he commented. "He said I must work boldly on and not think at all of what went wrong with me." In no time a confiding friendship developed, and Gachet on his side was one of the first to realize he was dealing with greatness. Vincent was painting at Gachet's house, and in a day or two he was painting the doctor's portrait (fig. 33). "Monsieur Gachet is absolutely *fanatical* about this portrait, and wants me to do one for him, if I can, exactly

like it . . . He has now got the length of understanding the last portrait of the Arlésienne . . ." "I shall probably do the portrait too of his daughter who is 19 years old . . ." This was good medicine for Vincent, even to Gachet's being "as discouraged about his job as a doctor as I about my painting . . ." "Altogether old Gachet is very like you and me." Even to appearance, as it happened, for Theo's wife noted the resemblance between the brothers and Gachet. "I have a portrait of Gachet with the heartbroken expression of our time." For this, blue tonalities were essential, and an anatomy which twisted and writhed. Gachet got Vincent to etch, and there is also an etching of the doctor.

Gachet invited Theo and his family for the day. It was the tenth of June. The day was idyllic, as it turned out. Vincent met his family at the station, with a bird's nest in hand for his nephew. A nest—vortex and cradle—Vincent had brought one home for his studio at Nuenen, years before. They all had lunch in the open air and went for a walk in the afternoon. It was the last day of its kind.

For the time being, Vincent, sustained by Dr. Gachet and with his own relations near-by in Paris, appeared equal to his environment. He lived in the midst of Auvers; his canvases were crowded with his participation in the world about him, a world of people and their nests. He had returned to humanity at least in his painting. In "Houses at Auvers" (plate XII) the gnarled forms of his art are congruous with the gnarled and genial age of the cottages;

and in place of the stark contrasts of the south, here are all the living subtleties in color of a watery climate. The painting is so successfully, so happily mastered, that one might hope that living had been mastered too.

Early in July Vincent was again in Paris at Theo's apartment, but this day was less fortunate. The child had been ill and the parents were tired and distraught. Theo was thinking for the hundredth time of leaving Goupil's and setting up for himself. Impractically, Vincent had often urged this in the past, but now the financial threat was all too clear. Anxiety over money lit up a conflict of loves and interests. Vincent felt that Theo's whole stock of paintings—not his own merely—was inadequately housed and protected. Theo's wife was thinking first of the needs of her child. In the midst of this, painter friends came to see Vincent. There was Aurier, whom he had known before in Paris, had just written a critical article on him. This recognition in print upset Vincent. Toulouse Lautrec appeared and stayed to lunch, and joked with Vincent about an undertaker they had met on the stairs. Still another friend was due; but Vincent, overwrought, hurried back to Auvers.

His painting now reflected his new insecurity with which he was unable to deal. For his insecurity was based on reality, and it was a reality beyond his control. He was reasonable, but he knew his limitations. "... *putting aside all ambition*," wrote Vincent, "we can live together for years without ruining each other."

Jo sent him an encouraging letter which seemed to lift his anxiety and he set to work again harder than ever. To be sure there was a new nagging lack of money, for his luggage had just arrived from Arles. No question of a studio yet, for the furniture in Arles was as good as lost. Thoughts of a painters' union again, but vague and half-hearted.

A sporadic letter to Gauguin, who had it in mind now to go to Madagascar. Vincent's painting grew more chaotic. Forms that spiralled at St. Rémy now were angular and broken. And there was something new in the handling. The parallel strokes took on a new aspect. The brushmarks were strangely like footprints of crowds milling, or running all one way across the canvas. During these days Vincent was pacing the fields in anxious conversation with himself.

His last canvas, "Crows over Wheatfield" (fig. 34), is so troubled, tumultuous, specter-haunted, with the black crows rising suddenly and a road lurching into nowhere in mid space, that there is still a sense of emergency to be met, as though the painter were still alive.

Vincent van Gogh shot himself on July 27, came home to his inn and lay down on his bed. Here his landlord found him and sent for Dr. Gachet. The doctor could not remove the bullet, and he sent for Theo who could not immediately be reached. Theo arrived the next day. Vincent lived until July 29, 1890. He was lucid, disheartened and content. He smoked his pipe. "I wish I could die now," he said, dying.

Theo had sent his wife and child to Holland a few days before and was about to join them on his vacation. This union was interrupted by the claims of a prior love.

Vincent was buried with his paintings on display about him, since he was attended by painters. And Dr. Gachet provided sunflowers.

Theo survived Vincent half a year. Their personalities interlocked, and for all that Theo had supported Vincent, Vincent also supported him. Theo's mind became affected, and he died in Holland, paralyzed and insane. But he was buried with his brother in Auvers.

SELECTED BIBLIOGRAPHY

Books on van Gogh in English

Barr, Alfred H. Jr. *Vincent van Gogh.* New York, Museum of Modern Art, 1935.

de Batz, George. *The Art and Life of Vincent van Gogh.* With an introduction by Dr. Alfred M. Frankfurter. New York, Wildenstein, 1943.

Burra, Peter. *Van Gogh.* (Great Lives, No. 29.) London, Duckworth, 1934.

de la Faille, J. B. *Vincent van Gogh; with a foreword by Charles Terrasse.* New York, French and European Publications, Inc., 1939. (Revision of *L'Œuvre de Vincent van Gogh: catalogue raisonné.* 4 vols. Paris and Brussels, van Oest, 1928.)

Earp, T. W. *Van Gogh.* London, T. Nelson and Sons.

Gogh, Vincent van. *The Letters of a Post-Impressionist; being the familiar correspondence of Vincent van Gogh.* Translated from the German with an introductory essay by A. M. Ludovici. London, Constable, 1912.
The Letters of Vincent van Gogh to his Brother, 1872-1886. With a memoir by his sister-in-law, J. van Gogh-Bonger. 2 vols. New York and Boston, Houghton Mifflin, 1927.
Further Letters of Vincent van Gogh to his Brother, 1886-1889. New York and Boston, Houghton Mifflin, 1929.
Letters to an Artist; from Vincent van Gogh to Anton ridder van Rappard, 1881-1885. Translated from the Dutch by Rela van Messel with an introduction by Walter Pach. New York, The Viking Press, 1936.
Letters to Emile Bernard. Edited and translated by Douglas Lord. New York, Museum of Modern Art, 1938.

James, Philip. *Van Gogh, 1853-1890.* Faber and Faber, 1948.

Jewell, Edwin Alden. *Vincent van Gogh.* New York, The Hyperion Press, 1946.

Meier-Graefe, Julius. *Vincent van Gogh: a biographical study.* 2 vols. London and Boston, The Medici Society, 1926. (First published 1922.)
Vincent van Gogh: a biographical study. New York, Payson and Clarke, 1928.
Vincent van Gogh: a biographical study. New York, Harcourt, Brace, 1933.

Muensterberger, W. *Vincent van Gogh: drawings, pastels, studies.* London, Falcon Press, 1947.

Pach, Walter. *Vincent van Gogh, 1853-1890.* New York, Artbook Museum, 1936.

du Quesne-van Gogh, Elisabeth H. *Personal Recollections of Vincent van Gogh.* With a foreword by Arthur B. Davies. New York and Boston, Houghton Mifflin, 1913.

Rich, Daniel Catton; Rousseau, Theodore Jr. *Van Gogh, paintings and drawings.* New York, The Metropolitan Museum of Art, The Art Institute of Chicago, 1949.

Schapiro, Meyer. *Vincent van Gogh,* New York, H. N. Abrams, 1950.

Scherjon, W. and de Gruyter, Jos. *Vincent van Gogh's Great Period: Arles, St. Rémy and Auvers sur Oise,* Amsterdam, "De Spieghel" Ltd., 1937.